UNITED STATES OF AMERICA COLORING BOOK

M.L. Gutierrez

ISBN: 1717511732
ISBN-13: 978-1717511737

E PLURIBUS UNUM

TABLE OF CONTENTS

Alabama

State Name:	Alabama
Capital:	Montgomery
Abbreviations:	AL; Ala.
Nickname:	The Yellowhammer State
Other Names:	The Heart of Dixie; The Cotton State
Motto:	We dare to defend our rights
Statehood:	December 14, 1819 (22nd)
Demonym:	Alabaman; Alabamian
Time Zone:	Central Time Zone
Region/Div:	South / East South Central
Slogan:	Stars Fell On; Heart of Dixie; Sweet Home Alabama; Alabama: Like the Third World, but Closer!
Song:	"Alabama"
Name Origin:	From the Choctaw word albah amo meaning "thicket - clearers" or "plant - cutters."
Brief History:	The Spanish came during the 1600s and named the region La Florida. The area was claimed by the French from 1702 to 1763 as part of La Louisiane. It became part of British West Florida (1763 – 1783) when the French lost the Seven Years War to the British. In 1783, Great Britain ceded West Florida to Spain in the Treaty of Versailles. However, the British also ceded the area to the United States in the 1783 Treaty of Paris. In 1795, with the Treaty of Madrid, Spain ceded their claim to the area to the United States. The U.S. Congress created the Mississippi Territory on April 1798. Then Congress created the Alabama Territory out of the eastern half of the Mississippi Territory on March 3, 1817.

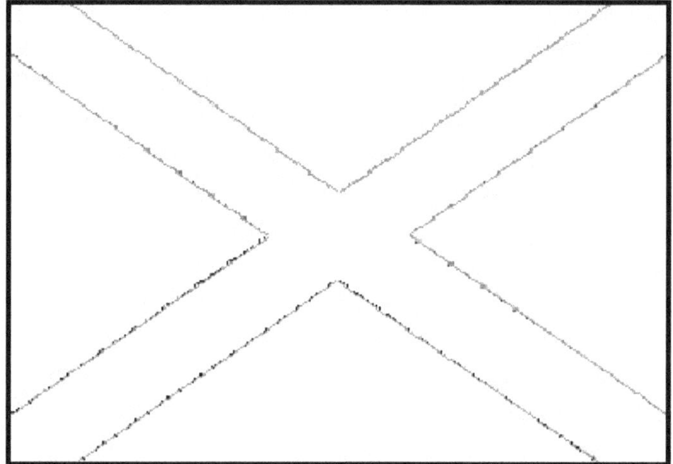

Flag

Seal

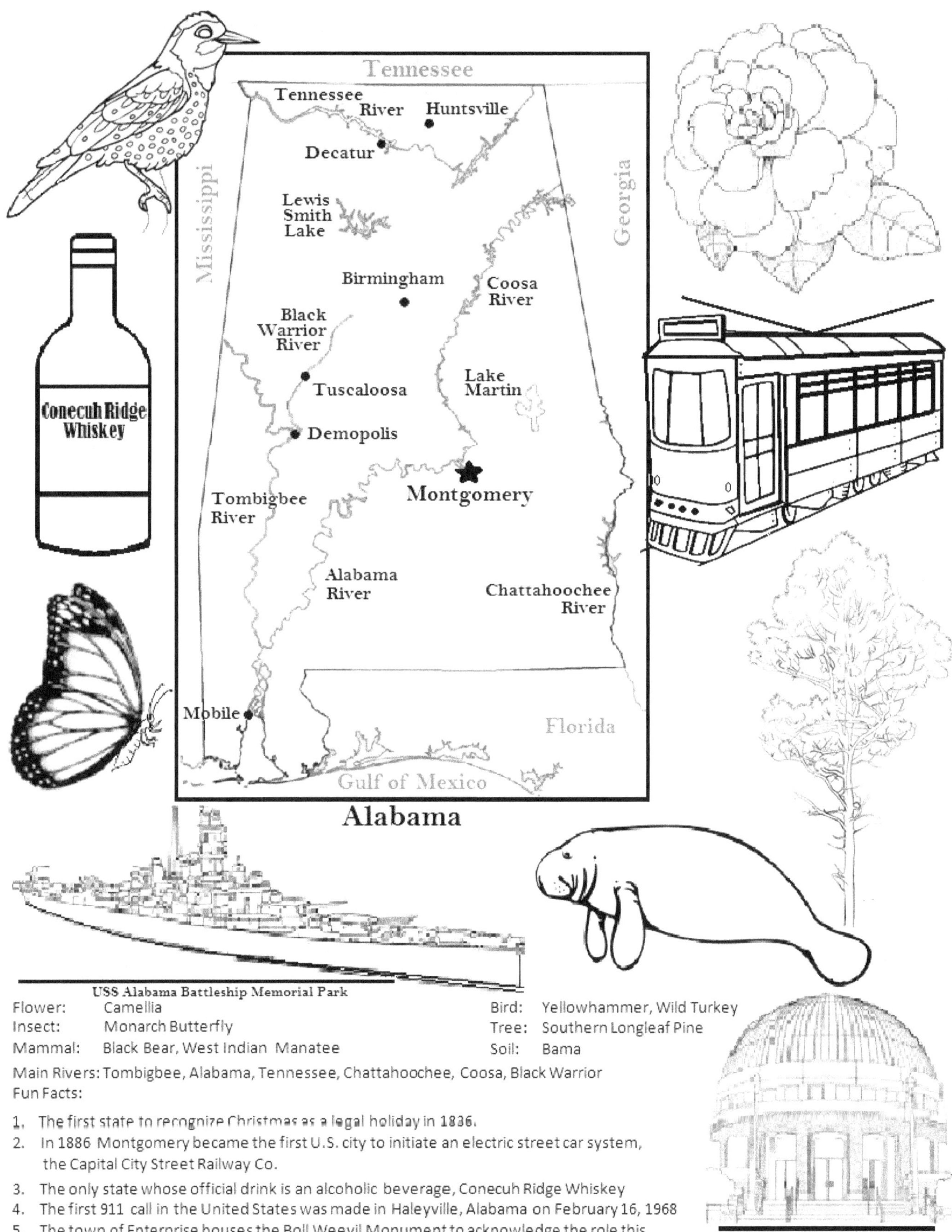

USS Alabama Battleship Memorial Park

Birmingham Civil Rights Institute

Flower:	Camellia	Bird:	Yellowhammer, Wild Turkey
Insect:	Monarch Butterfly	Tree:	Southern Longleaf Pine
Mammal:	Black Bear, West Indian Manatee	Soil:	Bama

Main Rivers: Tombigbee, Alabama, Tennessee, Chattahoochee, Coosa, Black Warrior

Fun Facts:

1. The first state to recognize Christmas as a legal holiday in 1836.
2. In 1886 Montgomery became the first U.S. city to initiate an electric street car system, the Capital City Street Railway Co.
3. The only state whose official drink is an alcoholic beverage, Conecuh Ridge Whiskey
4. The first 911 call in the United States was made in Haleyville, Alabama on February 16, 1968
5. The town of Enterprise houses the Boll Weevil Monument to acknowledge the role this destructive insect played in encouraging farmers to grow crops other than cotton.

Alaska

State Name:	Alaska
Capital:	Juneau
Abbreviations:	AK; Alas.
Nickname:	The Last Frontier
Other Names:	Land of the Midnight Sun; Sourdough State; North Star State; Seward's Ice Box; Johnson's Polar Bear Garden
Motto:	North to the Future
Statehood:	January 3, 1959 (49th)
Demonym:	Alaskan
Time Zone:	Alaska Standard Time; Hawaii-Aleutian Standard Time
Region/Div:	West / Pacific
Slogan:	The Great Land; The Last Frontier; Beyond Your Dreams, Within Your Reach
Song:	"Alaska's Flag"
Name Origin:	Corruption of Aleut word "aláxsxaq" meaning "great land" or "that which the sea breaks against"
Brief History:	The United States bought Alaska from the Russian Empire on March 30, 1867, for 7.2 million U.S. dollars. It became organized as a territory on May 11, 1912.

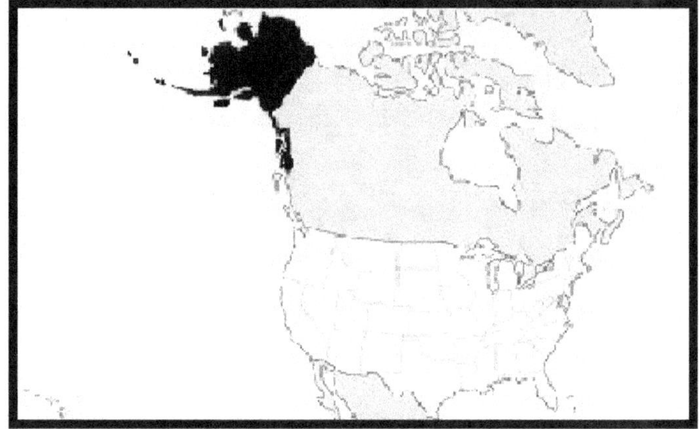

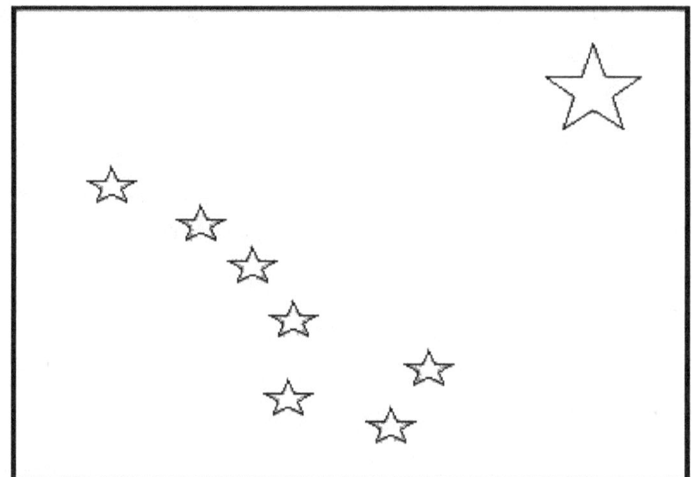

Flag

Seal

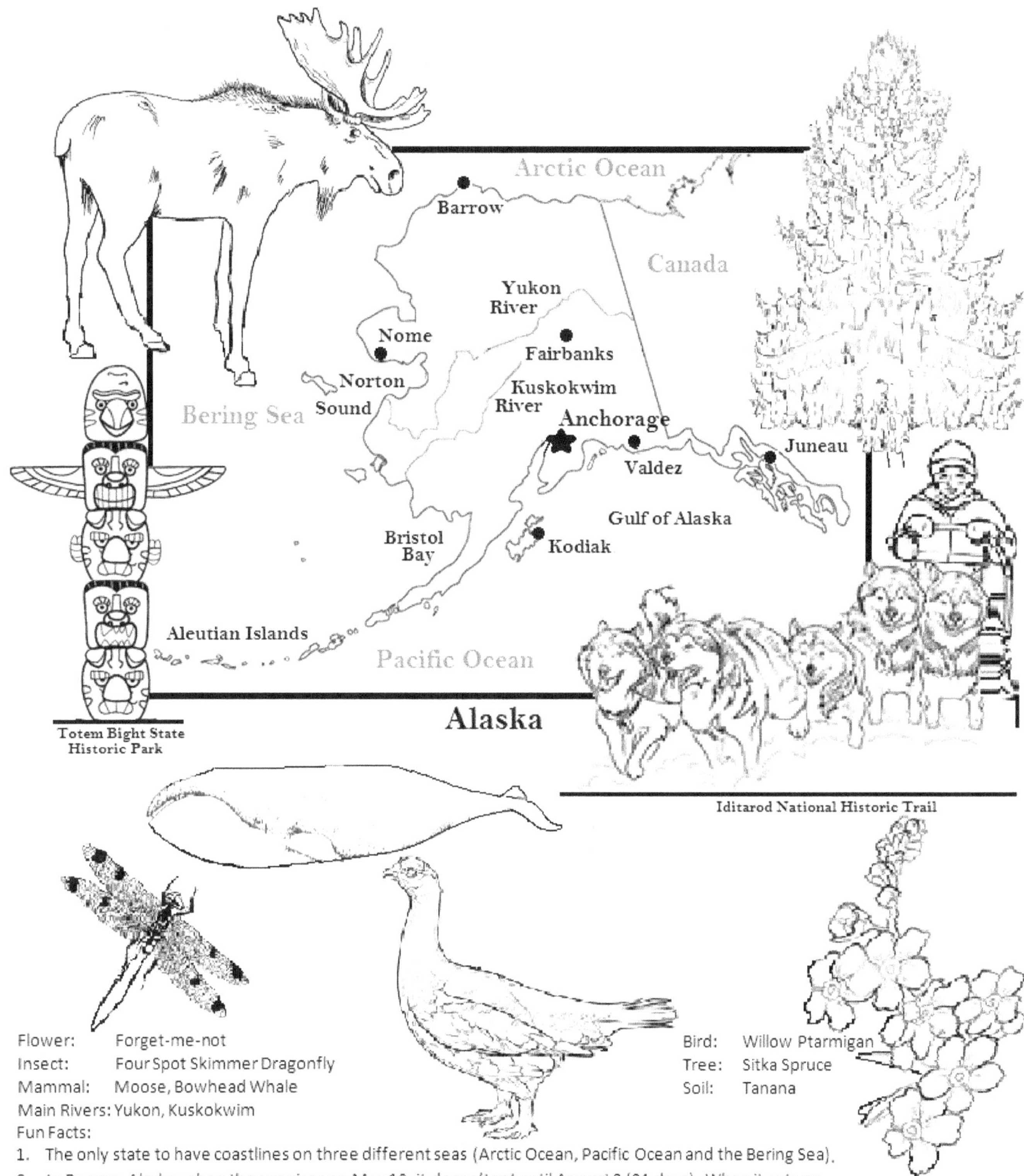

Flower: Forget-me-not
Insect: Four Spot Skimmer Dragonfly
Mammal: Moose, Bowhead Whale
Main Rivers: Yukon, Kuskokwim

Bird: Willow Ptarmigan
Tree: Sitka Spruce
Soil: Tanana

Fun Facts:

1. The only state to have coastlines on three different seas (Arctic Ocean, Pacific Ocean and the Bering Sea).
2. In Barrow, Alaska, when the sun rises on May 10, it doesn't set until August 2 (84 days). When it sets on November 18, Barrow residents do not see the sun again until January 24th (67 days).
3. Point Barrow, Alaska is northernmost point in all U.S. territory.
4. The 1925 serum run to Nome, also known as the Great Race of Mercy, was a transport of diphtheria antitoxin by dog sled relay across the U.S. territory of Alaska. Since 1973, the memory of the serum run has lived on in the Iditarod Trail Sled Dog Race held each March and is run on some of the same trails beaten by Balto, Togo and dozens of other sled dogs in a furious race against time.
5. Alaska has most official languages of any state in the US - English and 20 indigenous languages.

Arizona

State Name:	Arizona
Capital:	Phoenix
Abbreviations:	AZ; Ariz.
Nickname:	The Grand Canyon State
Other Names:	Apache State; Copper State
Motto:	God enriches
Statehood:	December 14, 1912 (48th)
Demonym:	Arizonan
Time Zone:	Mountain Standard Time; Only the Navajo Nation uses Daylight Saving Time
Region/Div:	South / East South Central
Slogan:	Grand Canyon State
Song:	"Arizona"
Name Origin:	From an earlier Spanish name, Arizonac, derived from the O'odham name alĭ ṣonak, meaning "small spring"
Brief History:	The Treaty of Guadalupe Hidalgo (1848) ended the Mexican-American War and called for Mexico to cede a portion of its land to the United States for $15 million. The ceded portion included all of present-day Arizona north of the Gila River. Then on December 30, 1853, the Gadsden Purchase agreement was signed. By 1855, the land between the two countries had been marked and all of Arizona, with the boundaries we know today, became part of the American territory. Arizona is the last state to join the union in the contiguous United States.

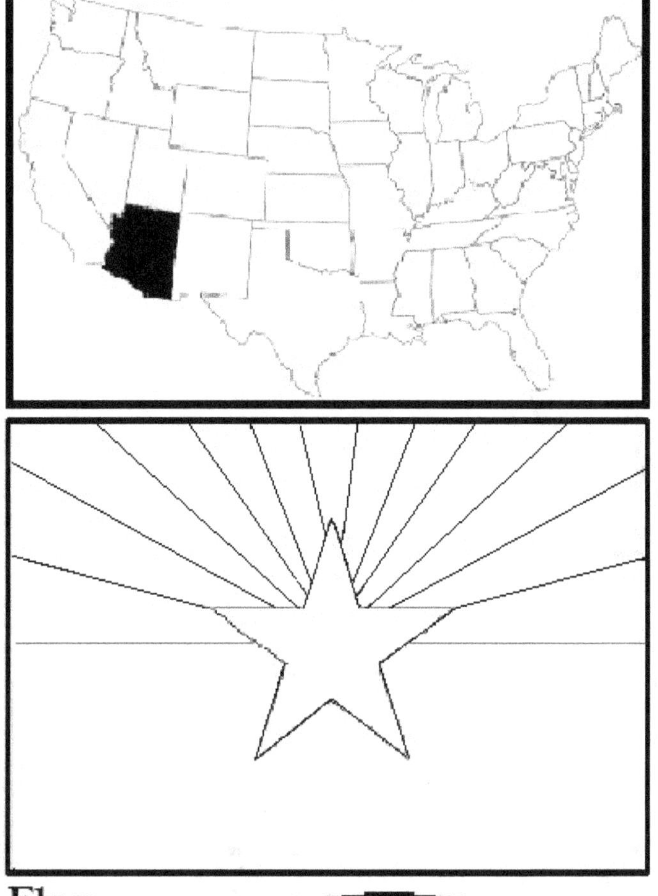

Flag

Seal

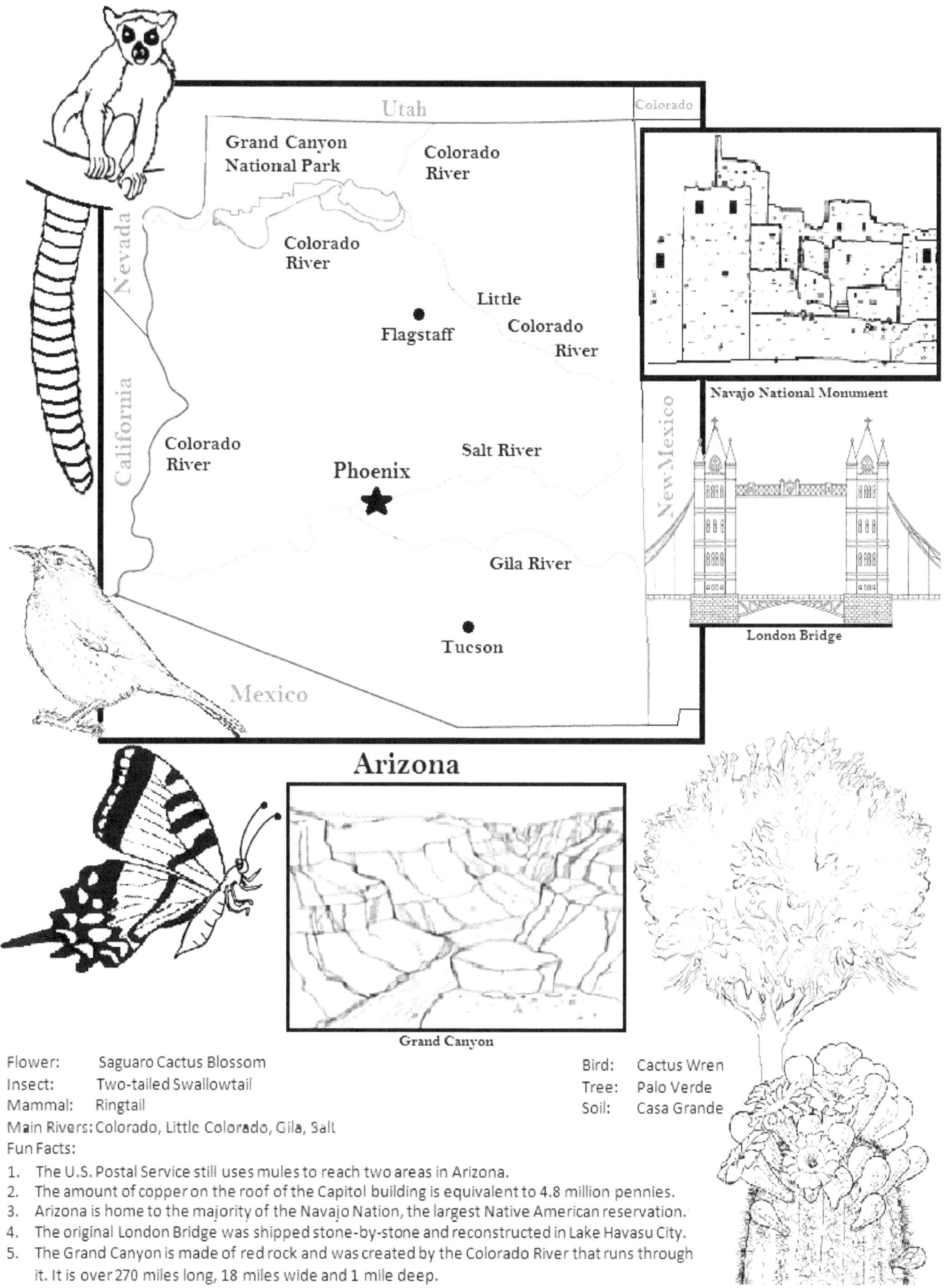

Arizona

Flower: Saguaro Cactus Blossom
Insect: Two-tailed Swallowtail
Mammal: Ringtail

Bird: Cactus Wren
Tree: Palo Verde
Soil: Casa Grande

Main Rivers: Colorado, Little Colorado, Gila, Salt

Fun Facts:

1. The U.S. Postal Service still uses mules to reach two areas in Arizona.
2. The amount of copper on the roof of the Capitol building is equivalent to 4.8 million pennies.
3. Arizona is home to the majority of the Navajo Nation, the largest Native American reservation.
4. The original London Bridge was shipped stone-by-stone and reconstructed in Lake Havasu City.
5. The Grand Canyon is made of red rock and was created by the Colorado River that runs through it. It is over 270 miles long, 18 miles wide and 1 mile deep.

Arkansas

State Name:	Arkansas
Capital:	Little Rock
Abbreviations:	AR; Ark.
Nickname:	The Natural State
Other Names:	The Hot Springs State; The Hot Water State ; The Bowie State; The Razorback State
Motto:	The people rule
Statehood:	June 15, 1836 (25th)
Demonym:	Arkansan
Time Zone:	Central Standard Time
Region/Div:	South / West South Central
Slogan:	Opportunity Land; Land of Opportunity; The Natural State
Song:	"Arkansas"
Name Origin:	The word "Arkansas" itself is a French pronunciation ("Arcansas") of a Quapaw (a related "Kaw" tribe) word, akakaze, meaning "land of downriver people" or the Sioux word akakaze meaning "people of the south wind".
Brief History:	In 1541, Spanish explorer Hernando De Soto was the first European to set foot in Arkansas. French explorers Jacques Marquette and Louis Jolliet came in 1673, and Frenchmen Robert La Salle and Henri de Tonti in 1681. Tonti established Arkansas Post at a Quapaw village in 1686, making it the first European settlement in the territory. Napoleon Bonaparte sold French Louisiana to the United States in 1803, including all of Arkansas, in a transaction known today as the Louisiana Purchase. The region was organized as the Territory of Arkansaw on July 4, 1819, with the territory admitted to the United States as the state of Arkansas on June 15, 1836.

Flag

Seal

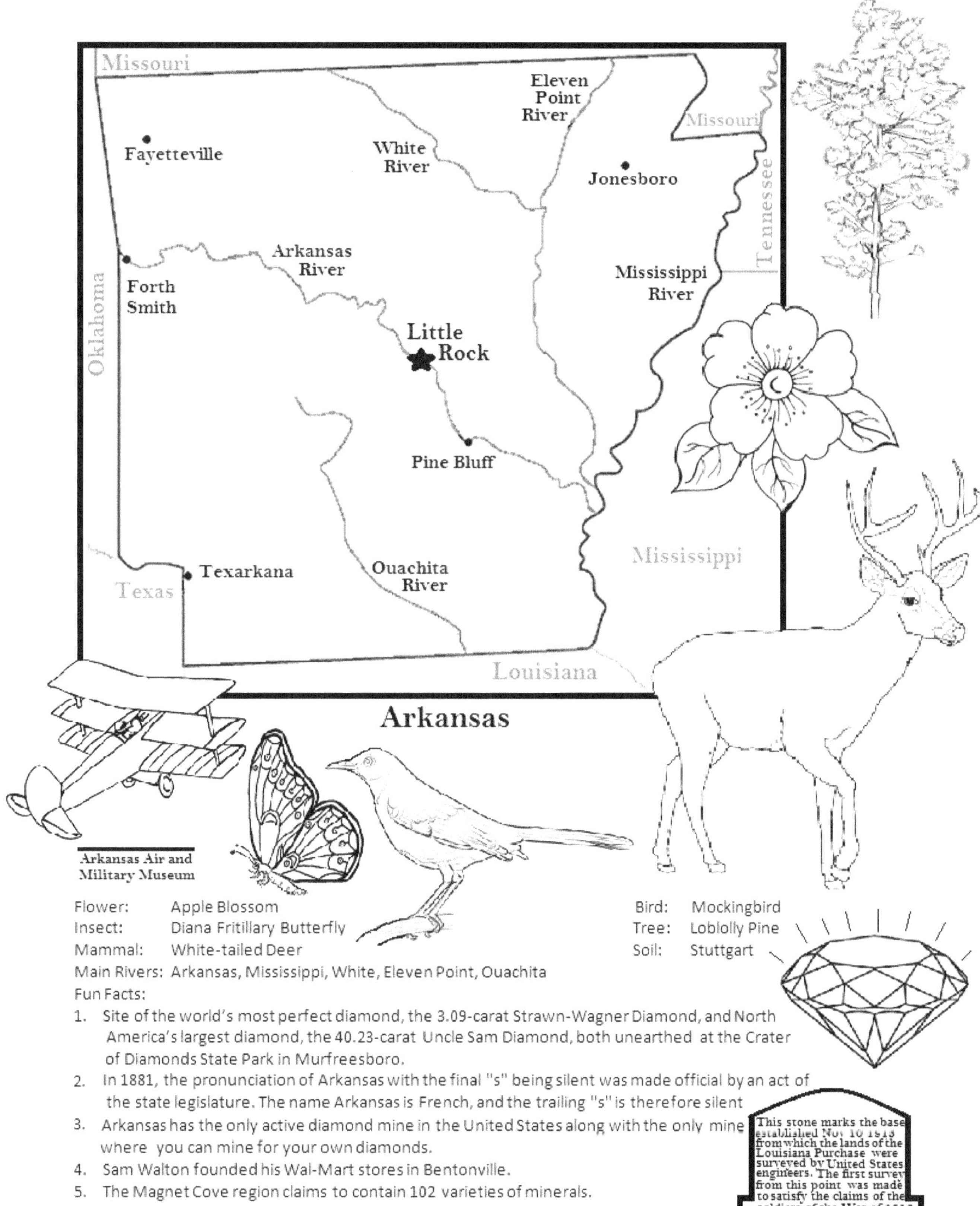

Flower: Apple Blossom
Insect: Diana Fritillary Butterfly
Mammal: White-tailed Deer

Bird: Mockingbird
Tree: Loblolly Pine
Soil: Stuttgart

Main Rivers: Arkansas, Mississippi, White, Eleven Point, Ouachita

Fun Facts:

1. Site of the world's most perfect diamond, the 3.09-carat Strawn-Wagner Diamond, and North America's largest diamond, the 40.23-carat Uncle Sam Diamond, both unearthed at the Crater of Diamonds State Park in Murfreesboro.
2. In 1881, the pronunciation of Arkansas with the final "s" being silent was made official by an act of the state legislature. The name Arkansas is French, and the trailing "s" is therefore silent
3. Arkansas has the only active diamond mine in the United States along with the only mine where you can mine for your own diamonds.
4. Sam Walton founded his Wal-Mart stores in Bentonville.
5. The Magnet Cove region claims to contain 102 varieties of minerals.

California

State Name:	California
Capital:	Sacramento
Abbreviations:	CA; Calif.
Nickname:	The Golden State
Other Names:	The Land of Milk and Honey; The El Dorado State; The Grape State
Motto:	I have found it
Statehood:	September 9, 1850 (31st)
Demonym:	Californian
Time Zone:	Pacific Standard Time
Region/Div:	West / Pacific
Slogan:	The Golden State
Song:	"I Love You California"
Name Origin:	California was the name given to a mythical island populated by Black Amazon warriors in the early 16th-century novel Las Sergas de Esplandián by Garci Rodríguez de Montalvo.
Brief History:	The Treaty of Guadalupe Hidalgo is the peace treaty signed on February 2, 1848, between the United States of America and the Mexican Republic, that ended the Mexican – American War (1846 – 1848). The treaty came into force on July 4, 1848. The treaty called for the U.S. to pay US$15 million to Mexico and to pay off the claims of American citizens against Mexico up to US$5 million. It gave the United States the Rio Grande as a boundary for Texas, and gave the U.S. ownership of California.

Flag

Seal

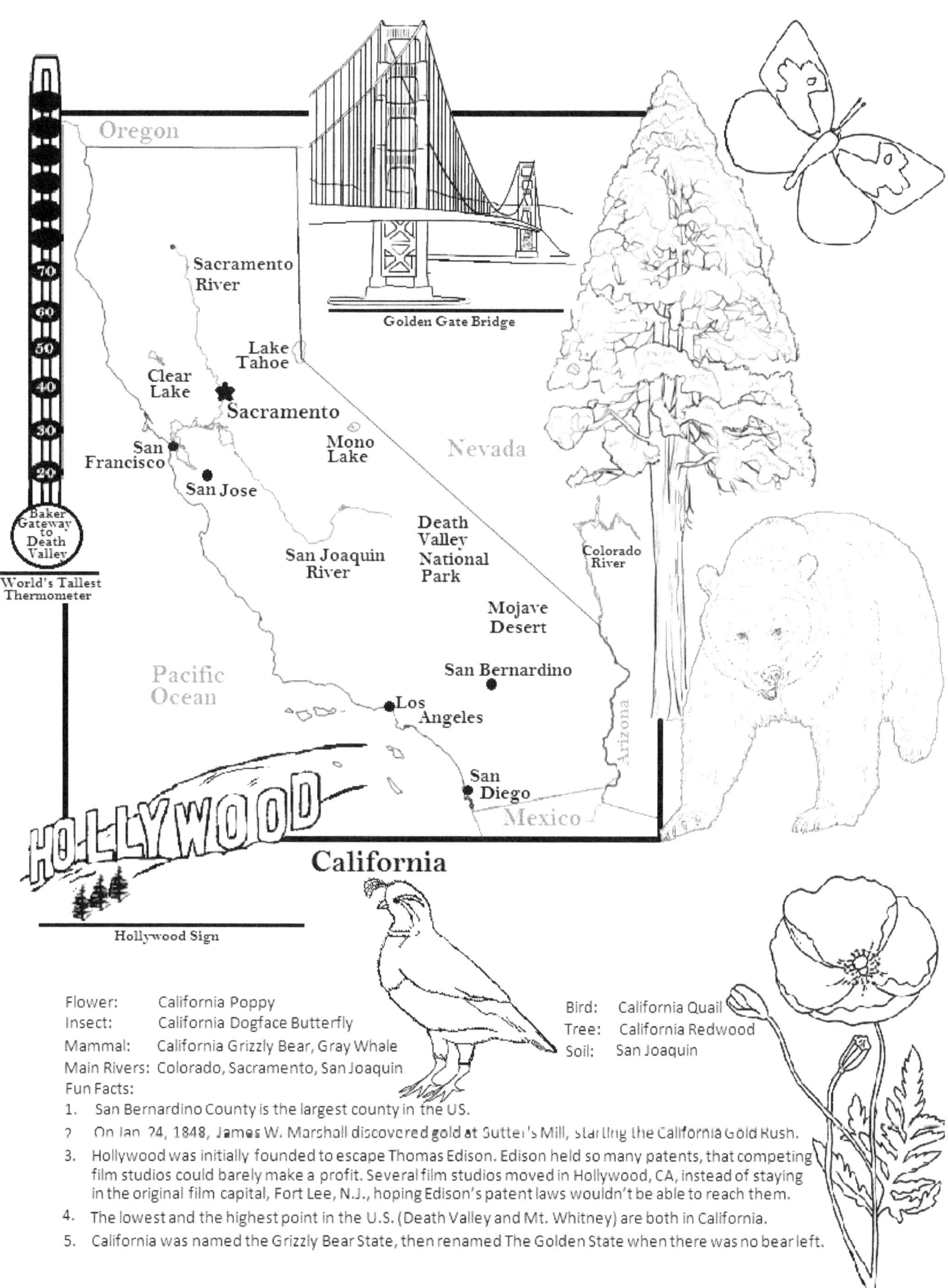

Flower: California Poppy
Insect: California Dogface Butterfly
Mammal: California Grizzly Bear, Gray Whale
Main Rivers: Colorado, Sacramento, San Joaquin
Fun Facts:

Bird: California Quail
Tree: California Redwood
Soil: San Joaquin

1. San Bernardino County is the largest county in the US.
2. On Jan 24, 1848, James W. Marshall discovered gold at Sutter's Mill, starting the California Gold Rush.
3. Hollywood was initially founded to escape Thomas Edison. Edison held so many patents, that competing film studios could barely make a profit. Several film studios moved in Hollywood, CA, instead of staying in the original film capital, Fort Lee, N.J., hoping Edison's patent laws wouldn't be able to reach them.
4. The lowest and the highest point in the U.S. (Death Valley and Mt. Whitney) are both in California.
5. California was named the Grizzly Bear State, then renamed The Golden State when there was no bear left.

Colorado

State Name:	Colorado
Capital:	Denver
Abbreviations:	CO; Colo.
Nickname:	The Centennial State
Other Names:	Colorful Colorado; Columbine State; Mile-high State; Highest State
Motto:	Nothing without Providence
Statehood:	August 1, 1876 (38th)
Demonym:	Coloradan
Time Zone:	Mountain Standard Time
Region/Div:	West / Mountain
Slogan:	Colorful Colorado
Song:	"Where the Columbines Grow"
Name Origin:	From the Spanish word, "ruddy" or "reddish". The early Spanish explorers in the Rocky Mountain region named a river they found the Rio Colorado for its reddish silt. The name Colorado was chosen because it was commonly believed that the Colorado River originated in the territory.
Brief History:	First visited by Spanish explorers in the 1500s, the Spanish Empire claimed Colorado as part of its New Mexico province. In 1800, Spain ceded the area to France. The U.S. obtained eastern Colorado as part of the Louisiana Purchase in 1803, the central portion in 1845 with the admission of Texas as a state, and the western part in 1848 as a result of the Mexican War. By the Treaty of Guadalupe Hidalgo, Mexico ceded to United States most of that part of Colorado not acquired by Louisiana Purchase.

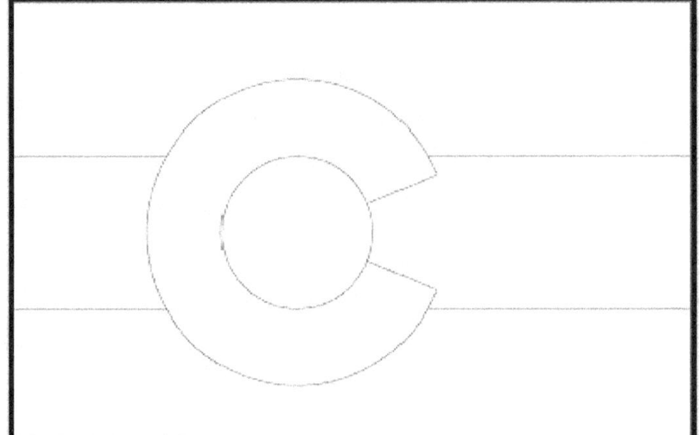

Flag

Seal

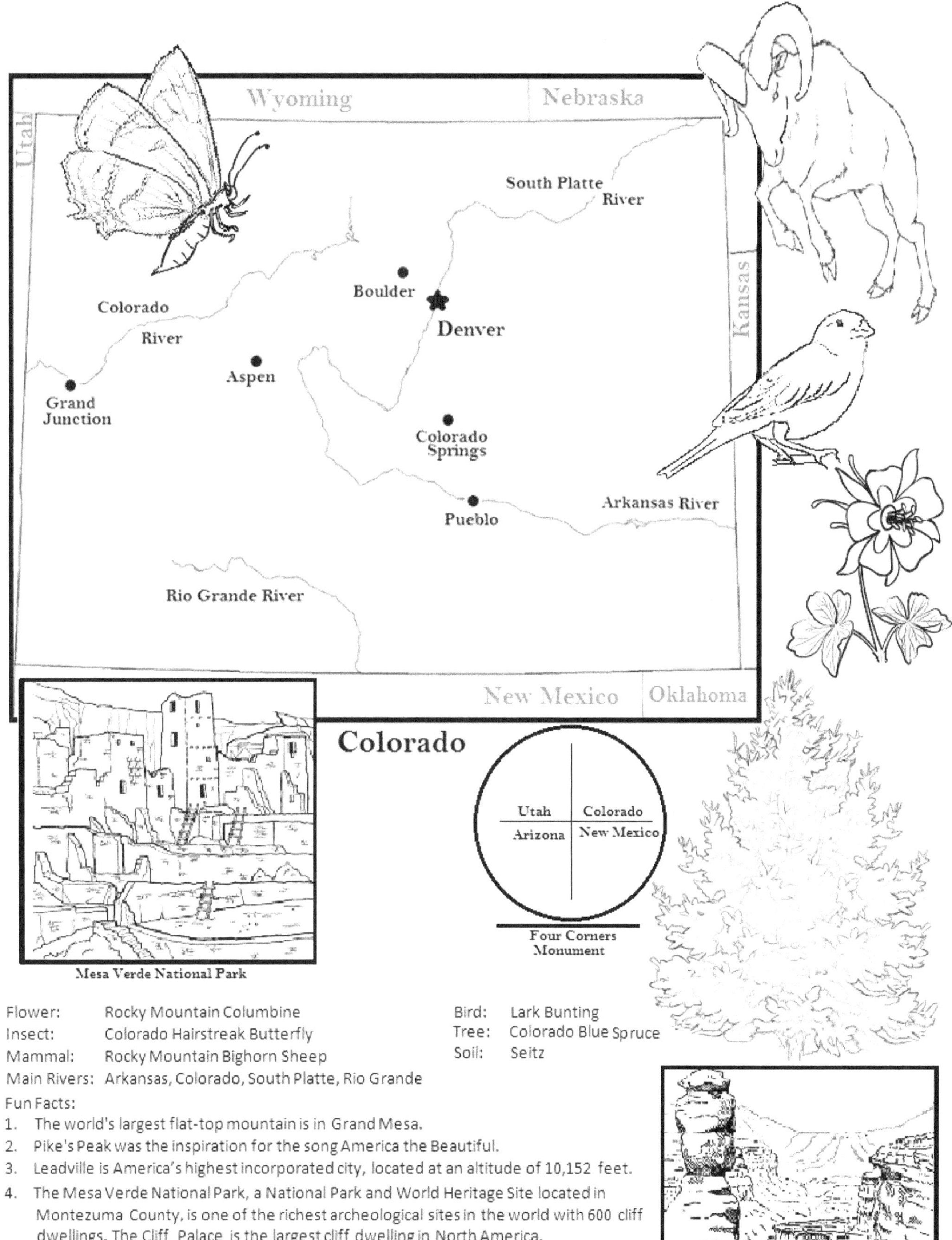

Colorado

Mesa Verde National Park

Flower: Rocky Mountain Columbine
Insect: Colorado Hairstreak Butterfly
Mammal: Rocky Mountain Bighorn Sheep
Main Rivers: Arkansas, Colorado, South Platte, Rio Grande

Bird: Lark Bunting
Tree: Colorado Blue Spruce
Soil: Seitz

Fun Facts:

1. The world's largest flat-top mountain is in Grand Mesa.
2. Pike's Peak was the inspiration for the song America the Beautiful.
3. Leadville is America's highest incorporated city, located at an altitude of 10,152 feet.
4. The Mesa Verde National Park, a National Park and World Heritage Site located in Montezuma County, is one of the richest archeological sites in the world with 600 cliff dwellings. The Cliff Palace is the largest cliff dwelling in North America.
5. The Dwight Eisenhower Memorial Tunnel between Clear Creek & Summit counties is the highest auto tunnel in the U.S. at 3,401 meters.

Colorado National Monument

Connecticut

State Name:	Connecticut
Capital:	Hartford
Abbreviations:	CT; Conn.
Nickname:	The Constitution State
Other Names:	The Nutmeg State; The Provisions State; The Land of Steady Habits
Motto:	He who transplanted still sustains
Statehood:	January 9, 1788 (5th)
Demonym:	Connecticuter
Time Zone:	Eastern Standard Time
Region/Div:	Northeast / New England
Slogan:	Constitution State; Full of Surprises
Song:	"Yankee Doodle"
Name Origin:	From an Indian word (Quinnehtukqut) meaning "beside the long tidal river."
Brief History:	Connecticut was one of the original thirteen colonies. In 1662, it became an official English colony. In 1775, The American Revolutionary War, between Great Britain and its Thirteen Colonies broke out. After the war, Connecticut worked with the other colonies to form a government. Connecticut ratified the new U.S. Constitution on January 9, 1788 and became the fifth state to join the United States.

Flag

Seal

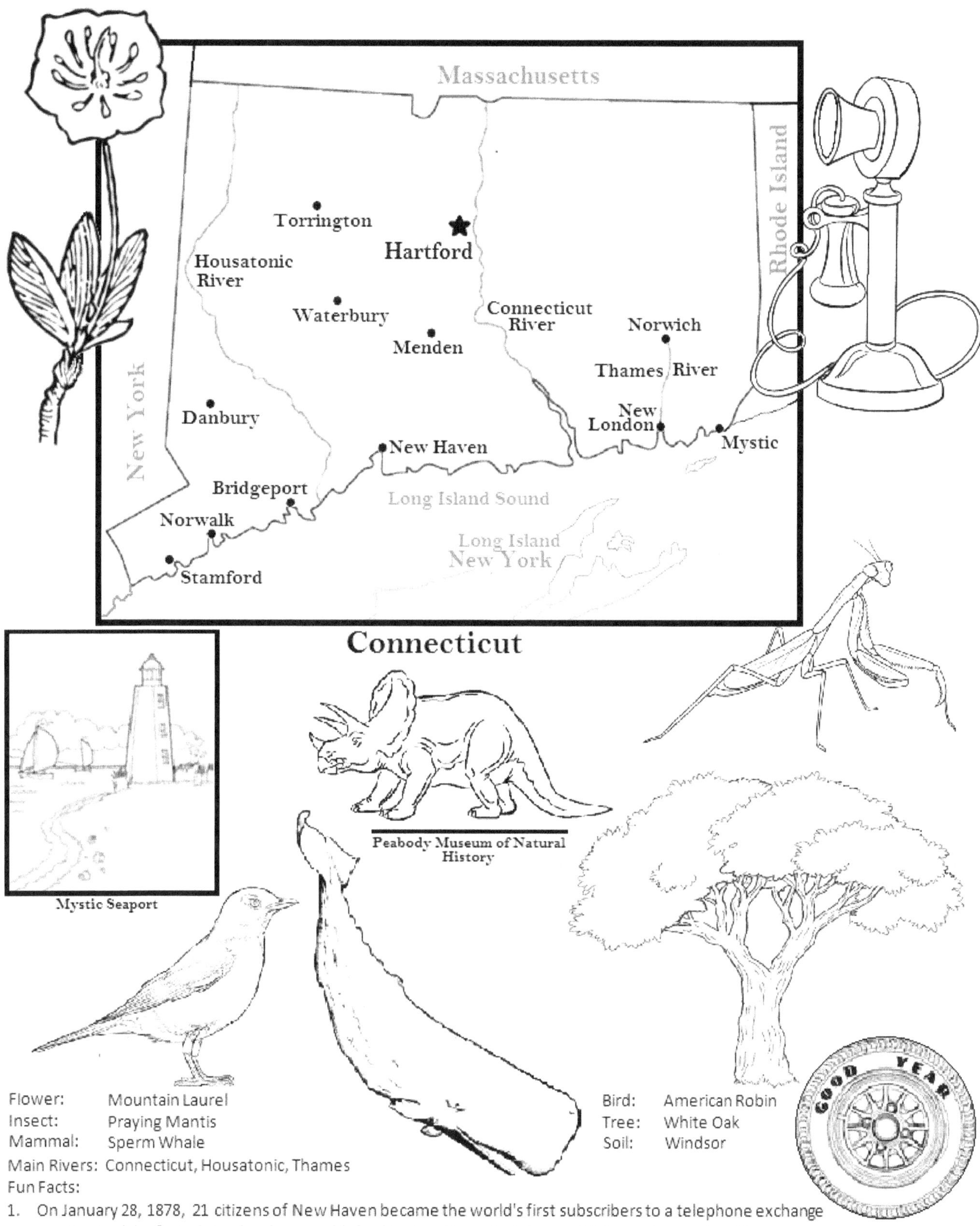

Connecticut

Mystic Seaport

Peabody Museum of Natural History

Flower: Mountain Laurel
Insect: Praying Mantis
Mammal: Sperm Whale
Main Rivers: Connecticut, Housatonic, Thames

Bird: American Robin
Tree: White Oak
Soil: Windsor

Fun Facts:

1. On January 28, 1878, 21 citizens of New Haven became the world's first subscribers to a telephone exchange service. And the first phone book was published in New Haven in February 1878, containing just 50 names.
2. West Hartford is the birthplace of Noah Webster, the author of the first dictionary published in 1807.
3. The first automobile law was passed by the state of CT in 1901. The speed limit was set at 12 miles per hour.
4. Connecticut is home to the oldest U.S. newspaper still being published: The Hartford Courant, established in 1764.
5. In 1843, Charles Goodyear invented the process for vulcanizing rubber.

Delaware

State Name:	Delaware
Capital:	Dover
Abbreviations:	DE; Del
Nickname:	The First State
Other Names:	Small Wonder;
	Blue Hen State;
	Diamond State;
	New Sweden
Motto:	Liberty and independence
Statehood:	December 7, 1787 (1st)
Demonym:	Delawarean
Time Zone:	Eastern Standard Time
Region/Div:	South / South Atlantic
Slogan:	It's Good Being First
Song:	"Our Delaware"
Name Origin:	From Delaware River and Bay; named in turn for Sir Thomas West, Baron De La Warr, the first English governor of Virginia. From de la werre, meaning "of the war" in Old French.
Brief History:	In 1631 the Dutch created a settlement called Zwaanendael. Within a year all the settlers were killed by the natives. In 1638, a Swedish settlement was established at Fort Christina (now in Wilmington). The colony lasted for 17 years. In 1651 the Dutch, reestablished a fort at present-day New Castle, and in 1655 they conquered the New Sweden colony. In 1664, the British took over the region from the Dutch. Delaware was one of the Thirteen Colonies which revolted against British rule in the American Revolution. Delaware was the first state to ratify the United States Constitution.

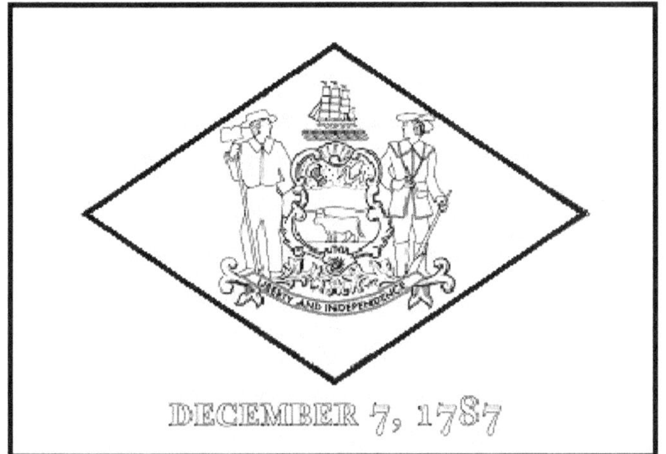

Flag

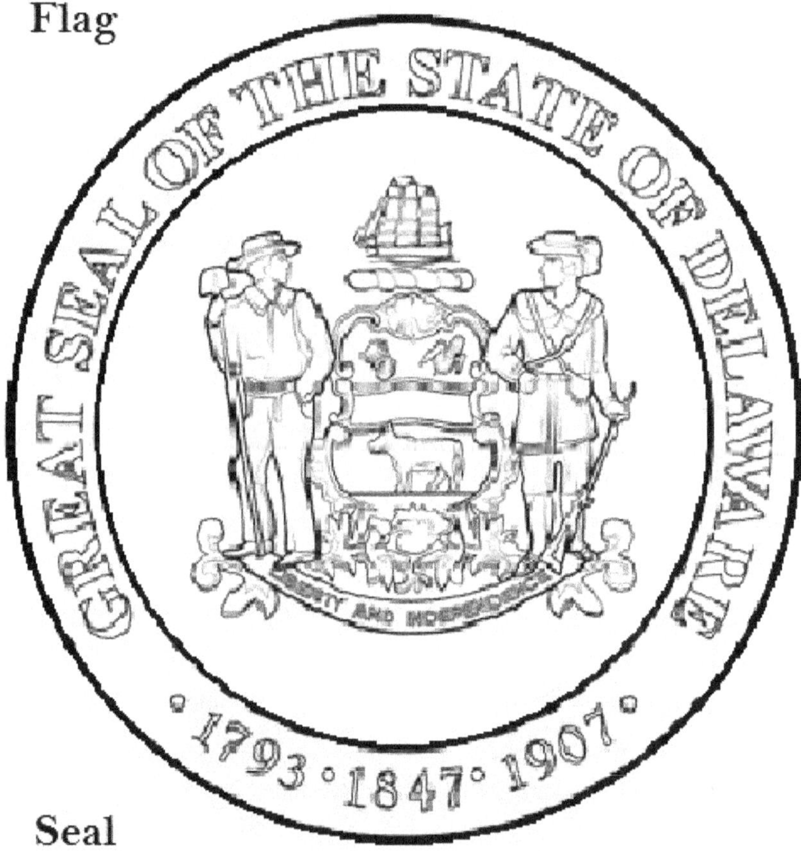

Seal

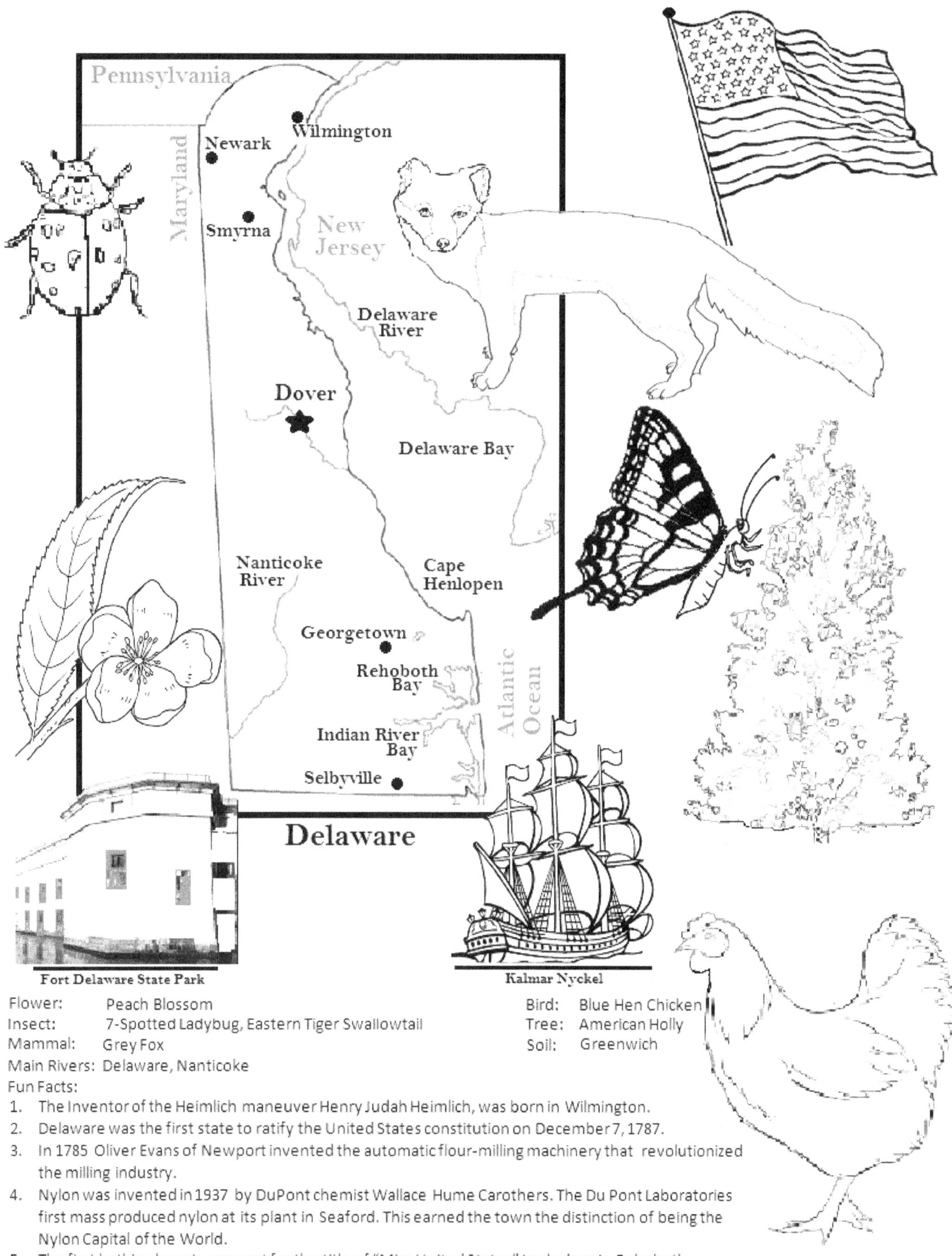

Fort Delaware State Park

Kalmar Nyckel

Flower: Peach Blossom
Insect: 7-Spotted Ladybug, Eastern Tiger Swallowtail
Mammal: Grey Fox
Main Rivers: Delaware, Nanticoke

Bird: Blue Hen Chicken
Tree: American Holly
Soil: Greenwich

Fun Facts:

1. The Inventor of the Heimlich maneuver Henry Judah Heimlich, was born in Wilmington.
2. Delaware was the first state to ratify the United States constitution on December 7, 1787.
3. In 1785 Oliver Evans of Newport invented the automatic flour-milling machinery that revolutionized the milling industry.
4. Nylon was invented in 1937 by DuPont chemist Wallace Hume Carothers. The Du Pont Laboratories first mass produced nylon at its plant in Seaford. This earned the town the distinction of being the Nylon Capital of the World.
5. The first bathing beauty pageant for the title of "Miss United States" took place in Rehoboth Beach in 1880. Inventor Thomas Edison was one of the contest's judges.

Florida

State Name:	Florida
Capital:	Tallahassee
Abbreviations:	FL; Fla.
Nickname:	The Sunshine State
Other Names:	Orange State; The Citrus State; Everglades State; Alligator State; The Peninsula State; The Flower State
Motto:	In God we trust
Statehood:	March 3, 1845 (27th)
Demonym:	Floridian, Floridan
Time Zone:	Eastern Standard Time; West of the Apalachicola River: Central Standard Time
Region/Div:	South / South Atlantic
Slogan:	Discover your own backyard: Florida; Visit Florida
Song:	"Old Folks at Home"
Name Origin:	Named for the day it was discovered (April 2, 1513) by Spanish explorer Ponce de Leon, who called it La Florida in honor of Pascua Florida, the Spanish Feast of the Flowers (Easter.)
Brief History:	Spanish conquistador Juan Ponce de León landed on the peninsula on April 2, 1513 and named the region Florida. In 1763, Spain traded Florida to the Kingdom of Great Britain for control of Havana, Cuba. Spain regained both East and West Florida after Britain's defeat in the American Revolution and the subsequent Treaty of Versailles in 1783. The Adams–Onís Treaty of 1819, which took effect in 1821 was a treaty between the United States and Spain that ceded Florida to the U.S.

Flag

Seal

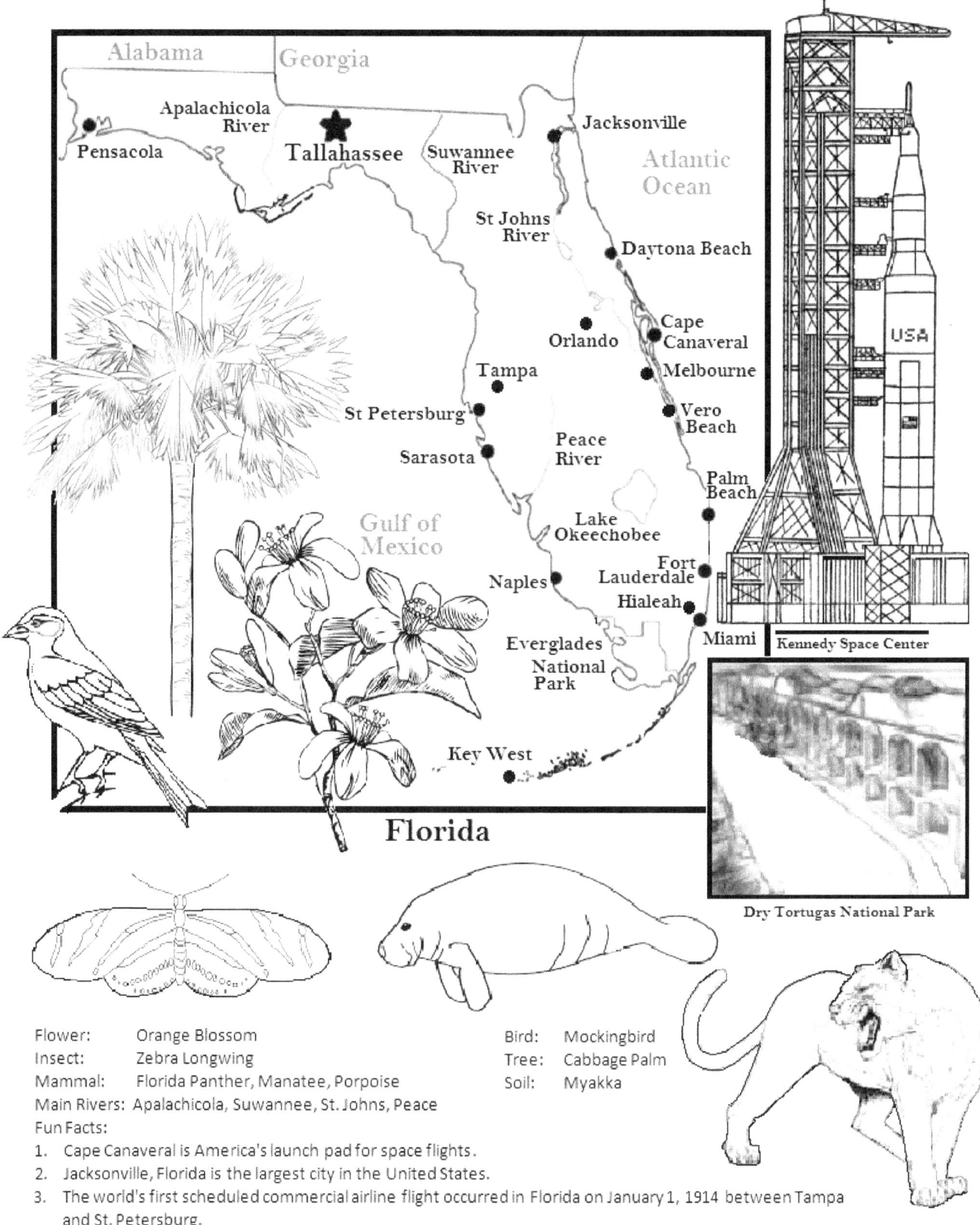

Flower: Orange Blossom
Insect: Zebra Longwing
Mammal: Florida Panther, Manatee, Porpoise
Main Rivers: Apalachicola, Suwannee, St. Johns, Peace

Bird: Mockingbird
Tree: Cabbage Palm
Soil: Myakka

Fun Facts:
1. Cape Canaveral is America's launch pad for space flights.
2. Jacksonville, Florida is the largest city in the United States.
3. The world's first scheduled commercial airline flight occurred in Florida on January 1, 1914 between Tampa and St. Petersburg.
4. The Florida Everglades is the only place on earth where crocodiles and alligators coexist in the wild.
5. St. Augustine lays claim to being the oldest city in the U.S. Founded in 1565 by Spanish explorers, it is the oldest continuously occupied European-established settlement within the borders of the continental United States.

Georgia

State Name:	Georgia
Capital:	Atlanta
Abbreviations:	GA; Ga.
Nickname:	The Peach State
Other Names:	Empire State of the South; Cracker State
Motto:	Wisdom, Justice and Moderation
Statehood:	January 2, 1788 (4th)
Demonym:	Georgian
Time Zone:	Eastern Standard Time
Region/Div:	South / South Atlantic
Slogan:	Georgia on My Mind
Song:	"Georgia on My Mind"
Name Origin:	Named after King George II of Great Britain
Brief History:	It began as a British colony in 1733. The colony was invaded by the Spanish in 1742, during the War of Jenkins' Ear. The Province of Georgia was one of the Thirteen Colonies that revolted against British rule in the American Revolution by signing the 1776 Declaration of Independence. Georgia declared its secession from the Union on January 19, 1861, and was one of the original seven Confederate states.

Flag

Seal

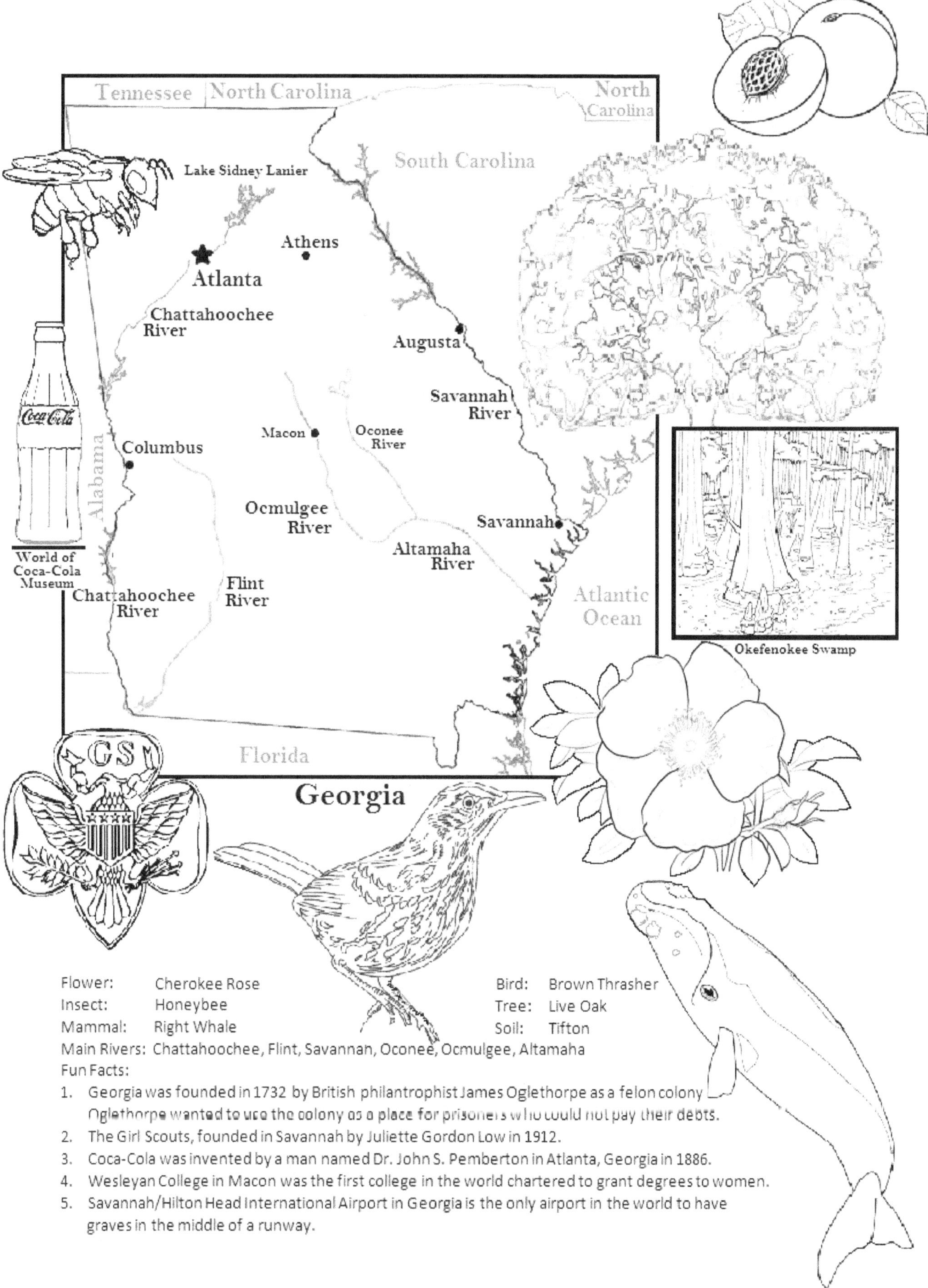

Flower: Cherokee Rose   Bird: Brown Thrasher
Insect: Honeybee   Tree: Live Oak
Mammal: Right Whale   Soil: Tifton
Main Rivers: Chattahoochee, Flint, Savannan, Oconee, Ocmulgee, Altamaha
Fun Facts:

1. Georgia was founded in 1732 by British philantrophist James Oglethorpe as a felon colony. Oglethorpe wanted to use the colony as a place for prisoners who could not pay their debts.
2. The Girl Scouts, founded in Savannah by Juliette Gordon Low in 1912.
3. Coca-Cola was invented by a man named Dr. John S. Pemberton in Atlanta, Georgia in 1886.
4. Wesleyan College in Macon was the first college in the world chartered to grant degrees to women.
5. Savannah/Hilton Head International Airport in Georgia is the only airport in the world to have graves in the middle of a runway.

Hawaii

State Name:	Hawaii
Capital:	Honolulu
Abbreviations:	HI; H.I.
Nickname:	The Aloha State
Other Names:	Paradise of the Pacific; The Islands of Aloha
Motto:	The life of the land is perpetuated in righteousness
Statehood:	August 21, 1959 (50th)
Demonym:	Hawaiian
Time Zone:	Hawaii-Aleutian Standard Time; Hawaii does not use Daylight Saving Time
Region/Div:	West / Pacific
Slogan:	"Hawaii Ponoi" (Hawai'i's Own)
Song:	"Hawaii Ponoi" (Hawai'i's Own)
Name Origin:	From Hawaiian Hawai'i, from Proto-Polynesian hawaiki, meaning "place of the Gods."; From the name of its largest island, Hawai'i, it was named for Hawai'iloa, a legendary figure from Hawaiian myth.
Brief History:	The Kingdom of Hawai'i was sovereign as a nation from 1810 until 1893 when the monarchy was overthrown by resident American and European landholders. It became an independent republic from 1894 until March 1959, Congress passed the Hawaii Admission Act, which U.S. President Dwight D. Eisenhower signed into law, officially making it a territory of the United States.

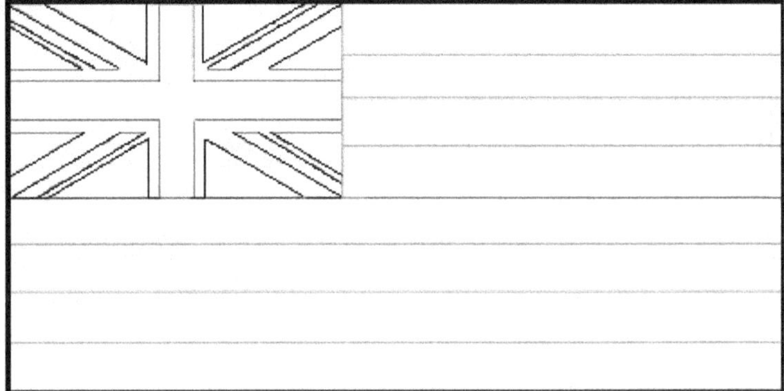

Flag

Seal

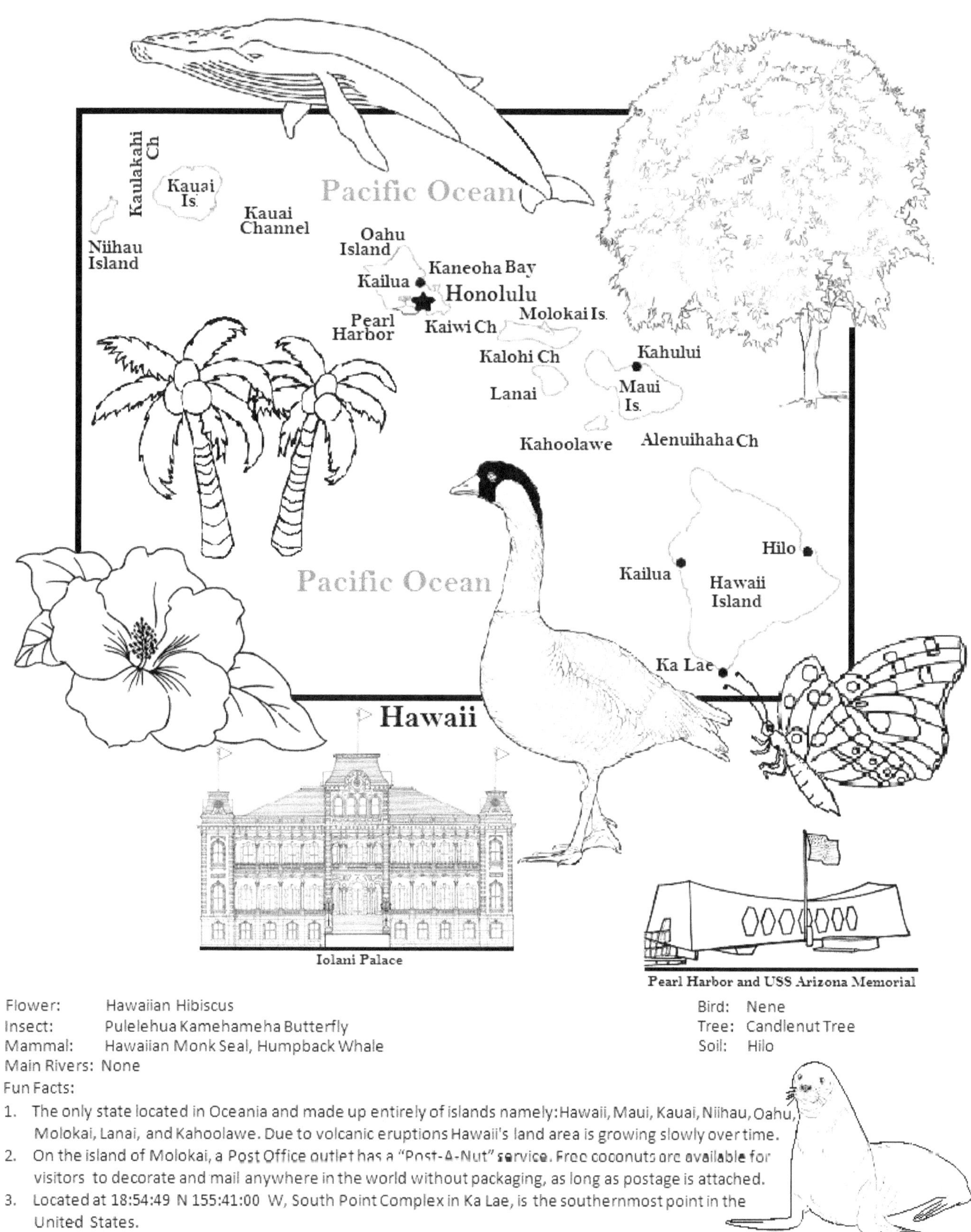

Iolani Palace

Pearl Harbor and USS Arizona Memorial

Flower: Hawaiian Hibiscus
Insect: Pulelehua Kamehameha Butterfly
Mammal: Hawaiian Monk Seal, Humpback Whale
Main Rivers: None

Bird: Nene
Tree: Candlenut Tree
Soil: Hilo

Fun Facts:

1. The only state located in Oceania and made up entirely of islands namely: Hawaii, Maui, Kauai, Niihau, Oahu, Molokai, Lanai, and Kahoolawe. Due to volcanic eruptions Hawaii's land area is growing slowly over time.
2. On the island of Molokai, a Post Office outlet has a "Post-A-Nut" service. Free coconuts are available for visitors to decorate and mail anywhere in the world without packaging, as long as postage is attached.
3. Located at 18:54:49 N 155:41:00 W, South Point Complex in Ka Lae, is the southernmost point in the United States.
4. Hawaii is the most isolated population center on the face of the earth. Hawaii is 2,390 miles from California; 3,850 miles from Japan; 4,900 miles from China; and 5,280 miles from the Philippines.
5. There are only 12 letters in the Hawaiian alphabet. Vowels: A, E, I, O, U Consonants: H, K, L, M, N, P, W.

Idaho

State Name:	Idaho
Capital:	Boise
Abbreviations:	ID; Ida.
Nickname:	The Gem State
Other Names:	Gem of the Mountains; Land of Famous Potatoes; Spud State
Motto:	"Esto Perpetua" (Let it be Perpetual)
Statehood:	July 3, 1890 (43rd)
Demonym:	Idahoan
Time Zone:	Mountain Standard Time; North of the Salmon River: Pacific Standard Time
Region/Div:	West / Mountain
Slogan:	Vacation Wonderland; World Famous Potatoes; Tasty Destinations
Song:	"Here We Have Idaho"
Name Origin:	Political lobbyist George Willing alleged Idaho meant "gem of the mountains" or "the sun comes from the mountains" in the Shoshone language. However, Willing eventually admitted that he just made up the word "Idaho."
Brief History:	For many years, the region that included Idaho was claimed by both the United States and Britain. In 1846, the area officially became part of the United States through the Oregon Treaty with Britain. It joined the Oregon Territory in 1848. In 1853, Idaho became part of the Washington Territory. In 1863, Idaho became its own territory called Idaho Territory.

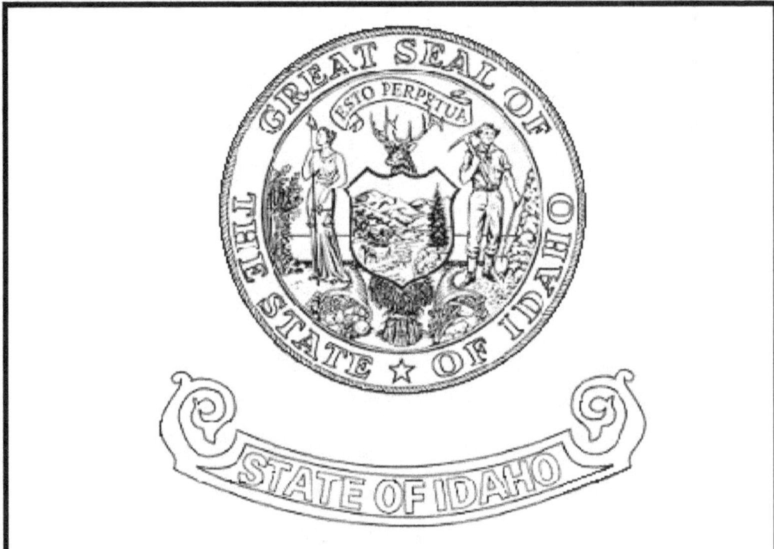

Flag

Seal

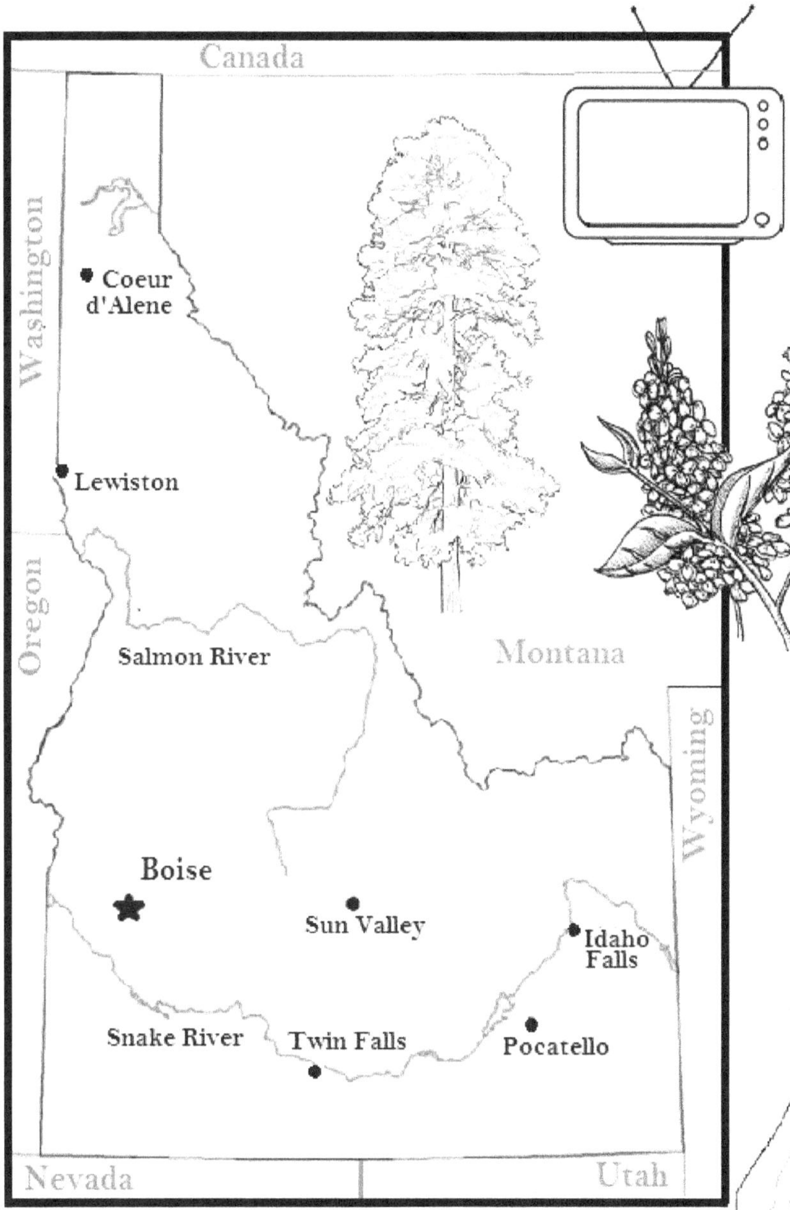

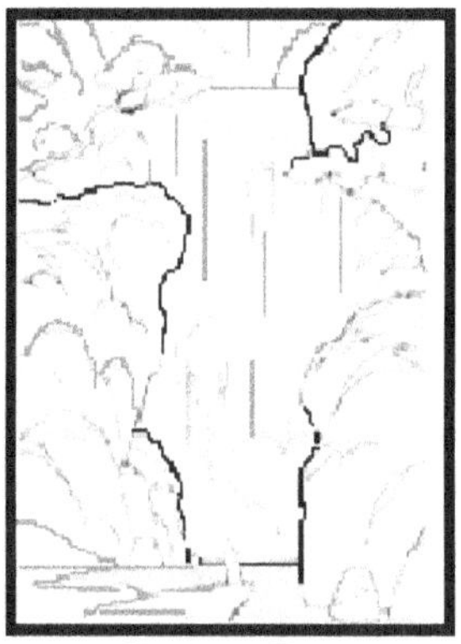

Idaho

Shoshone Falls

Flower: Syringa
Insect: Monarch Butterfly
Mammal: Appaloosa Horse
Main Rivers: Salmon, Snake

Bird: Mountain Bluebird
Tree: Western White Pine
Soil: Threebear

Fun Facts:

1. The deepest river gorge in North America is Idaho's Hells Canyon (7,993 ft. deep).
2. Seven Devils' Peaks, one of the highest mountain ranges in Idaho, Includes Heaven's Gate Lookout, where sightseers can look into four states. Heaven's Gate lookout offers an incredible view of portions of Washington, Oregon, Idaho, and Montana.
3. Rigby is known as the birthplace of television since it is Philo T. Farnsworth's hometown. Farnsworth pioneered television technology.
4. The Great Seal of Idaho was designed in 1890 by Mrs. Emma Edwards Green. It is the only Great Seal in the 50 states to be designed by a woman.
5. Shoshone Falls, a waterfall on the Snake River, is known as the Niagara Of The West. It drops 212 feet (65 meters) high — 45 feet (14 meters) higher than Niagara Falls — and flows over a rim nearly 1,000 feet (300 meters) wide.

Sun Valley Resort

Illinois

State Name:	Illinois
Capital:	Springfield
Abbreviations:	IL; Ill.
Nickname:	The Prairie State
Other Names:	Land of Lincoln; Corn State; Prairie State
Motto:	State Sovereignty, National Union
Statehood:	December 3, 1818 (21st)
Demonym:	Illinoisian; Illinoisan
Time Zone:	Eastern Standard Time; Northwest and southwest corners: Central Standard Time
Region/Div:	Midwest / East North Central
Slogan:	Land of Lincoln; Mile After Magnificent Mile; Right Here. Right Now.
Song:	"Illinois"
Name Origin:	The state of Illinois was named after the Illinois River. Illinois is Algonquin for "tribe of superior men".
Brief History:	During the late 1700s the French founded a mission at the Grand Village of the Illinois in Illinois Country and several forts in the area. Illinois was part of first New France, and then of La Louisiane until 1763, when it was ceded to the British after the Seven Years' War. The British reserved the territory for the Indians and then part of the British Province of Quebec. In 1778, George Rogers Clark claimed Illinois County for Virginia. In 1783, Virginia ceded the area to the new United States and it became part of the Northwest Territory. The Illinois Territory was created on February 3, 1809, with its capital at Kaskaskia. In early 1818, the General Assembly of the Illinois Territory sent a petition to the United States Congress asking to be admitted into the Union.

Flag

Seal

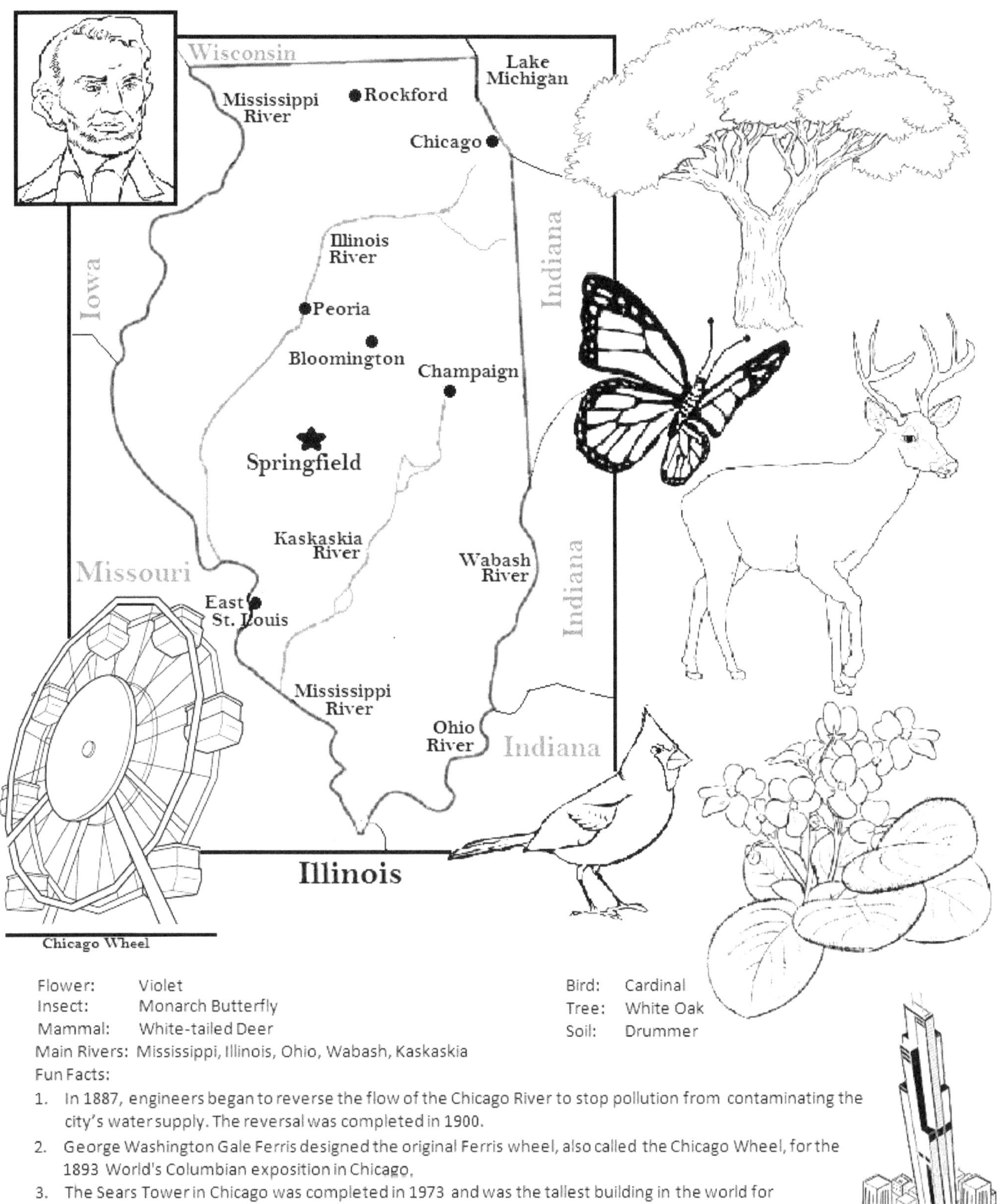

Flower: Violet
Insect: Monarch Butterfly
Mammal: White-tailed Deer
Bird: Cardinal
Tree: White Oak
Soil: Drummer

Main Rivers: Mississippi, Illinois, Ohio, Wabash, Kaskaskia

Fun Facts:

1. In 1887, engineers began to reverse the flow of the Chicago River to stop pollution from contaminating the city's water supply. The reversal was completed in 1900.

2. George Washington Gale Ferris designed the original Ferris wheel, also called the Chicago Wheel, for the 1893 World's Columbian exposition in Chicago.

3. The Sears Tower in Chicago was completed in 1973 and was the tallest building in the world for twenty-five years. Four states can be seen from the very top observation point of this Chicago landmark.

4. At 8 ft. 11.1 inches tall, Robert Pershing Wadlow, born in Alton, Illinois in 1918 holds the record as the tallest man in recorded history.

5. Before Abraham Lincoln was elected president he served in the Illinois legislature and practiced law in Springfield.

Indiana

State Name:	Indiana
Capital:	Indianapolis
Abbreviations:	IN; Ind.
Nickname:	The Hoosier State
Other Names:	Crossroads of America; Hospitality State
Motto:	The Crossroads of America
Statehood:	December 11, 1816 (19th)
Demonym:	Indianian; Hoosier
Time Zone:	Eastern Standard Time; Northwest and southwest corners: Central Standard Time
Region/Div:	Midwest / East North Central
Slogan:	Heritage State; Hoosier Hospitality; Honest-to-Goodness Indiana
Song:	"On the Banks of the Wabash, Far Away"
Name Origin:	"Land of the Indians", or simply "Indian Land"
Brief History:	During the 1700s, the French and the British came in the area. Fights between the French and British occurred and the British won in 1763. The French ceded all their lands to the British crown. In 1763, the British designated some land for Indian use and called it Indian Territory. In the 1783 Treaty of Paris, the British crown ceded their claims to the land to the newly formed United States. In 1787 the present-day Indiana became part of the Northwest Territory. In 1800 the region was renamed the Indiana territory when Ohio became a state and Indiana was reduced to its current size and geography. The legislature petitioned the U.S. Congress to make Indiana a state in 1815 and Indiana was accepted.

Flag

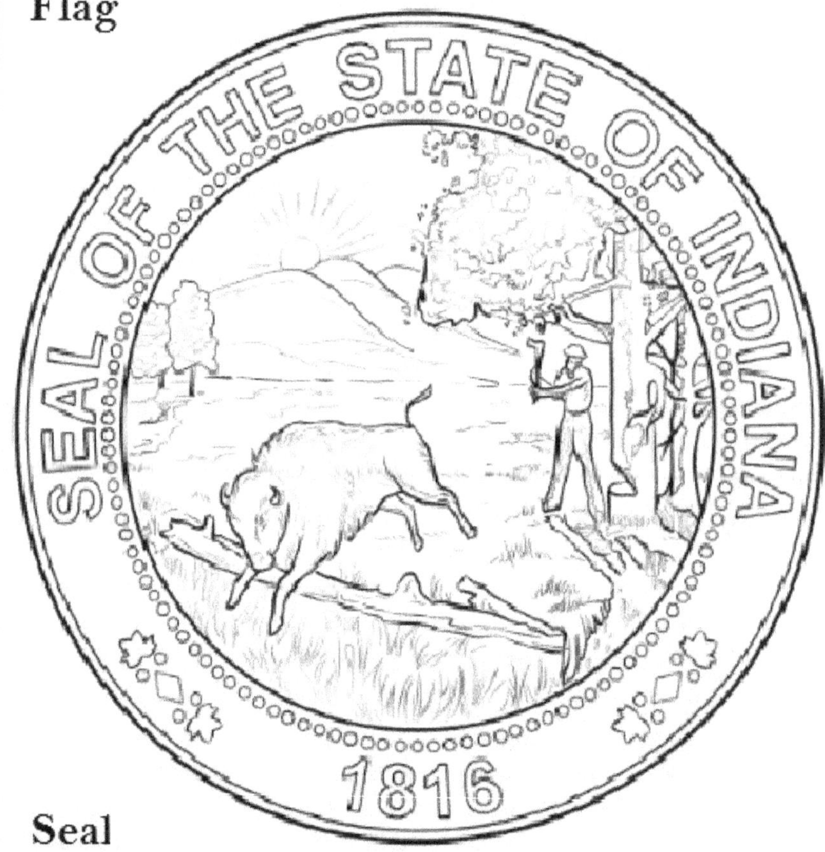

Seal

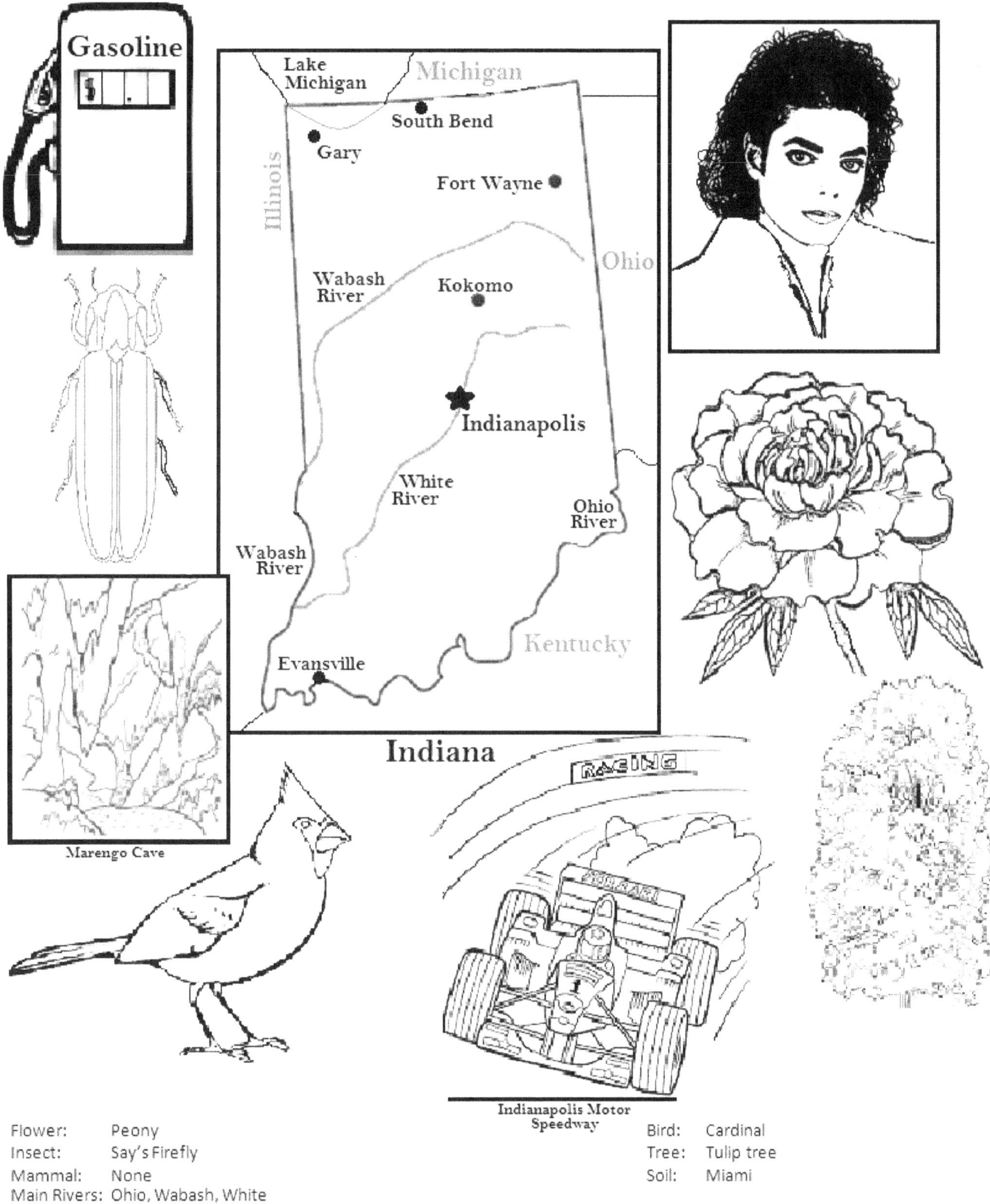

Flower:	Peony
Insect:	Say's Firefly
Mammal:	None
Main Rivers:	Ohio, Wabash, White

Bird:	Cardinal
Tree:	Tulip tree
Soil:	Miami

Fun Facts:

1. In 1862, Richard Gatling, of Indianapolis, invented the Gatling gun, a rapid-fire machine gun.
2. Indiana has one of the richest deposits of high quality limestone found anywhere on earth.
3. The first long-distance auto race in the U. S. was held May 30, 1911, at the Indianapolis Motor Speedway.
4. The first gasoline pump was invented and sold by Sylvanus Bowser in Fort Wayne, Indiana on September 5, 1885.
5. Famous people born in Indiana include singer Michael Jackson, TV host David Letterman, and basketball legend Larry Bird.

Iowa

State Name:	Iowa
Capital:	Des Moines
Abbreviation:	IA
Nickname:	The Hawkeye State
Other Names:	Tall Corn State
Motto:	Our liberties we prize and our rights we will maintain
Statehood:	December 28, 1846 (29th)
Demonym:	Iowan
Time Zone:	Central Standard Time
Region/Div:	Midwest / West North Central
Slogan:	The Corn State
Song:	"The Song of Iowa"
Name Origin:	Derived its name from the Ioway people, one of the many Native American tribes that occupied the state at the time of European exploration.
Brief History:	In 1673, the French travelled and established their territory in the area of Iowa. In 1763, the French transferred ownership to Spain before their impending defeat from the natives. In 1800, Napoleon Bonaparte took control of Louisiana from Spain in the Third Treaty of San Ildefonso. In 1803 the United States acquired what is today the state of Iowa, through the Louisiana Purchase. Congress divided the Louisiana Purchase into two parts—the Territory of Orleans and the District of Louisiana. The latter, of which in was placed. Iowa was placed under United States jurisdiction of the Territory of Indiana, with William Henry Harrison.

Flag

Seal

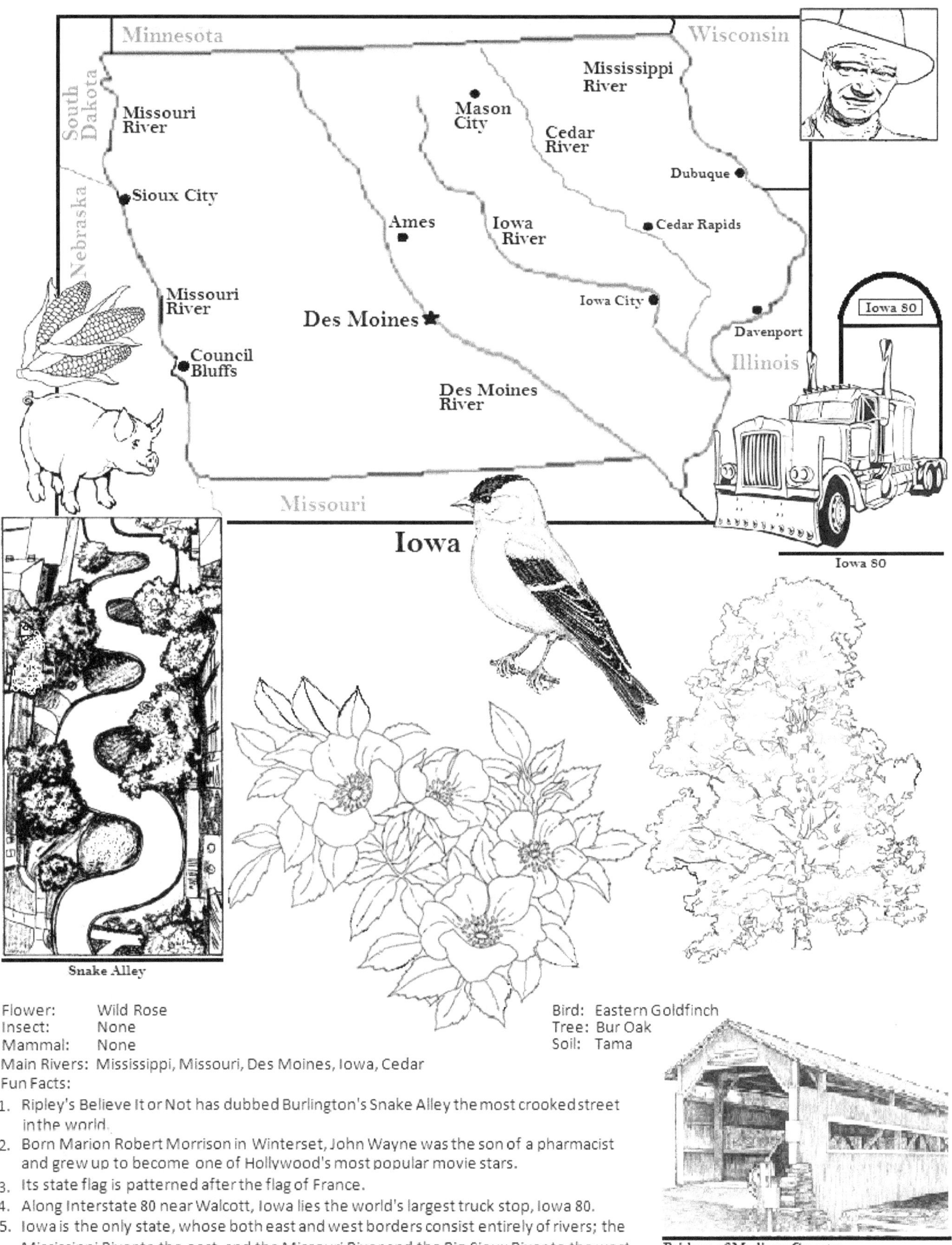

Flower: Wild Rose
Insect: None
Mammal: None

Bird: Eastern Goldfinch
Tree: Bur Oak
Soil: Tama

Main Rivers: Mississippi, Missouri, Des Moines, Iowa, Cedar

Fun Facts:

1. Ripley's Believe It or Not has dubbed Burlington's Snake Alley the most crooked street in the world.
2. Born Marion Robert Morrison in Winterset, John Wayne was the son of a pharmacist and grew up to become one of Hollywood's most popular movie stars.
3. Its state flag is patterned after the flag of France.
4. Along Interstate 80 near Walcott, Iowa lies the world's largest truck stop, Iowa 80.
5. Iowa is the only state, whose both east and west borders consist entirely of rivers; the Mississippi River to the east, and the Missouri River and the Big Sioux River to the west

Kansas

State Name:	Kansas
Capital:	Topeka
Abbreviations:	KS; Kan
Nickname:	The Sunflower State
Other Names:	The Wheat State; The Jayhawker State
Motto:	To the stars through difficulties
Statehood:	January 29, 1861 (34th)
Demonym:	Kansan
Time Zone:	Central Standard Time; Greeley, Hamilton, Sherman and Wallace counties: Mountain Standard Time
Region/Div:	Midwest / West North Central
Slogan:	The Wheat State; Midway USA
Song:	"Home on the Range"
Name Origin:	Named for the Kansa tribe, natively called kká:ze, meaning "people of the south wind."
Brief History:	In 1803, most of Kansas was acquired through the Louisiana Purchase. Southwest Kansas, was still a part of the Republic of Texas until the conclusion of the Mexican–American War in 1848, when these lands were ceded to the United States. From 1812 to 1821, Kansas was part of the Missouri Territory. The Kansas–Nebraska Act became law on May 30, 1854, establishing Nebraska Territory and Kansas Territory.

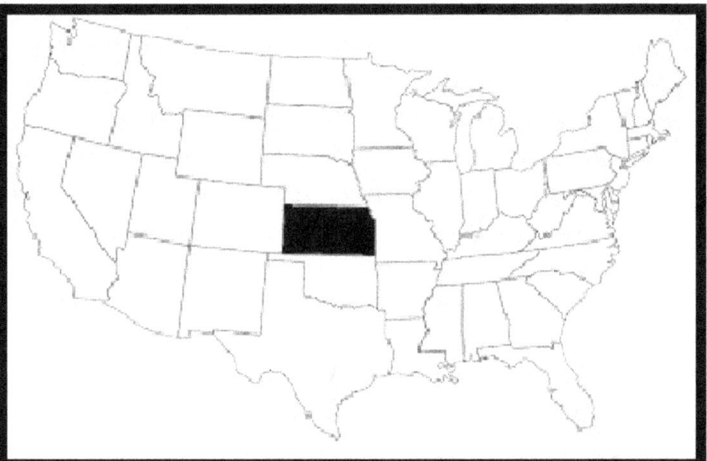

Flag

Seal

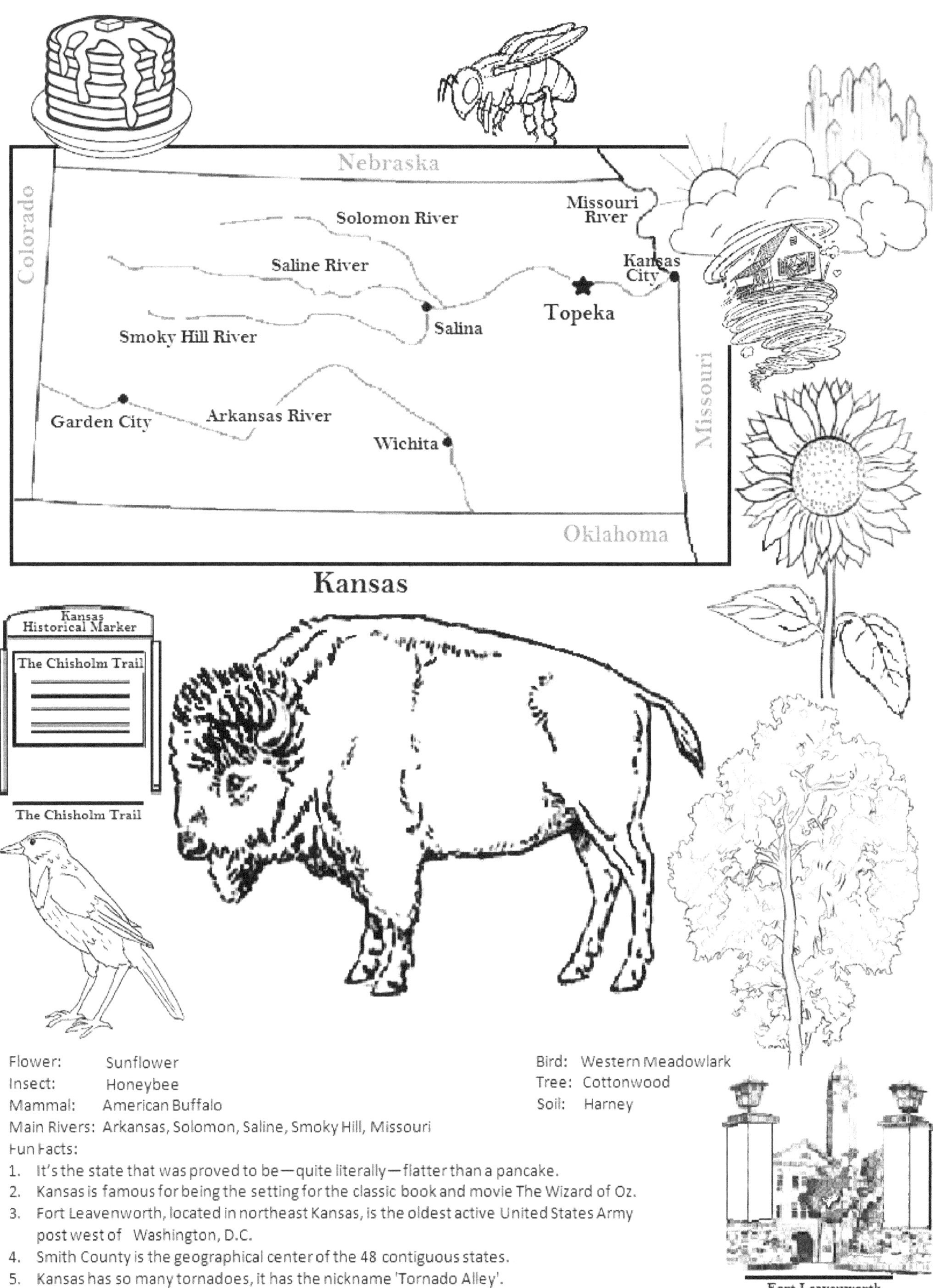

Flower: Sunflower
Insect: Honeybee
Mammal: American Buffalo
Bird: Western Meadowlark
Tree: Cottonwood
Soil: Harney

Main Rivers: Arkansas, Solomon, Saline, Smoky Hill, Missouri

Fun Facts:

1. It's the state that was proved to be—quite literally—flatter than a pancake.
2. Kansas is famous for being the setting for the classic book and movie The Wizard of Oz.
3. Fort Leavenworth, located in northeast Kansas, is the oldest active United States Army post west of   Washington, D.C.
4. Smith County is the geographical center of the 48 contiguous states.
5. Kansas has so many tornadoes, it has the nickname 'Tornado Alley'.

Fort Leavenworth

Kentucky

State Name:	Commonwealth of Kentucky
Capital:	Frankfort
Abbreviations:	KY; Ky.
Nickname:	The Bluegrass State
Other Names:	Hemp State;
	Tobacco State;
	Dark and Bloody Ground
Motto:	United we stand, divided we fall
Statehood:	June 1, 1792 (15th)
Demonym:	Kentuckian
Time Zone:	Central Standard Time;
	Eastern Standard Time
Region/Div:	South / East South Central
Slogan:	Bluegrass State;
	It's That Friendly;
	Unbridled Spirit
Song:	"My Old Kentucky Home"
Name Origin:	From the Iroquois word "ken-tah-ten," which means land
Brief History:	Originally a part of the Commonwealth of Virginia. In 1776, the region of Virginia beyond the Appalachian Mountains was established as Kentucky County by the Virginia General Assembly. In 1788 and in 1789, Virginia granted its consent to Kentucky's statehood. The United States Congress gave its approval on February 4, 1791.

Flag

Seal

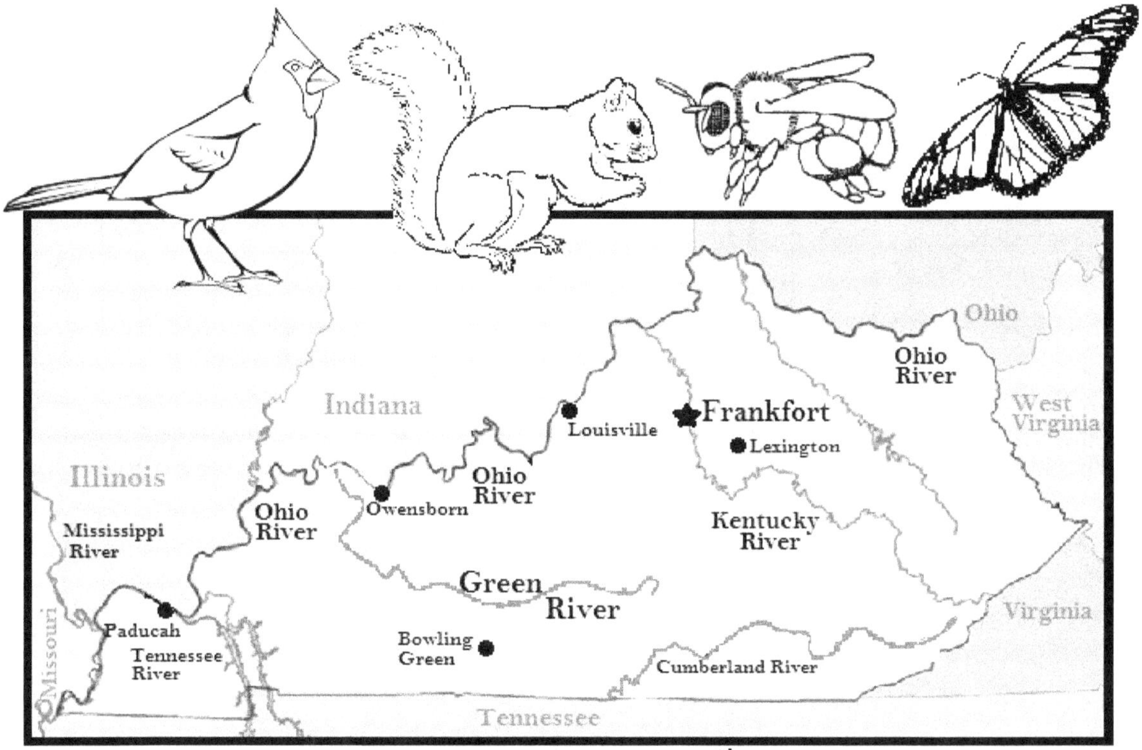

Kentucky

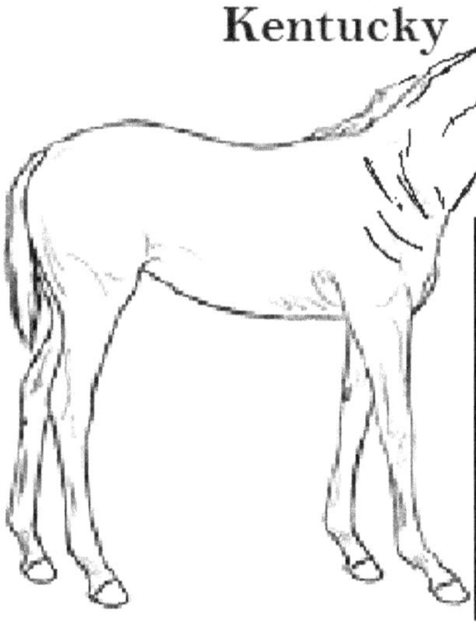

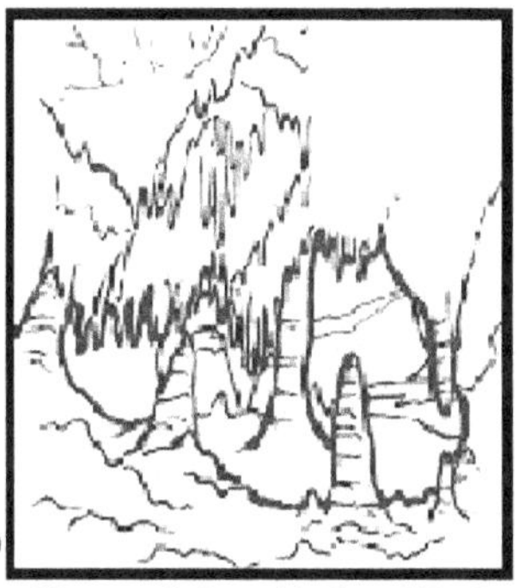

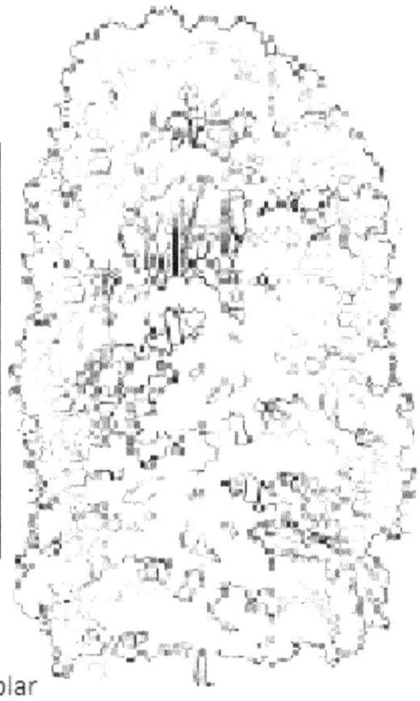

Flower: Goldenrod
Insect: Viceroy Butterfly, Honeybee
Mammal: Gray Squirrel, Thoroughbred Horse
Main Rivers: Mississippi, Ohio, Tennessee, Green, Kentucky, Cumberland

Bird: Cardinal
Tree: Tulip Poplar
Soil: Crider

Mammoth Cave National Park

Fun Facts:
1. The Kentucky Derby is the oldest horse race in the country held yearly every first Saturday of May since 1875.
2. Colonel Sanders began selling the first Kentucky Fried Chicken in Corbin, Kentucky on the side of the road
3. Mammoth Cave is the longest cave system in the world.
4. The public saw an electric light for the first time in Louisville when Thomas Edison introduced an incandescent light bulb to crowds at the Southern Exposition in 1883.
5. Middlesboro is the only city in the United States built within a meteor crater.

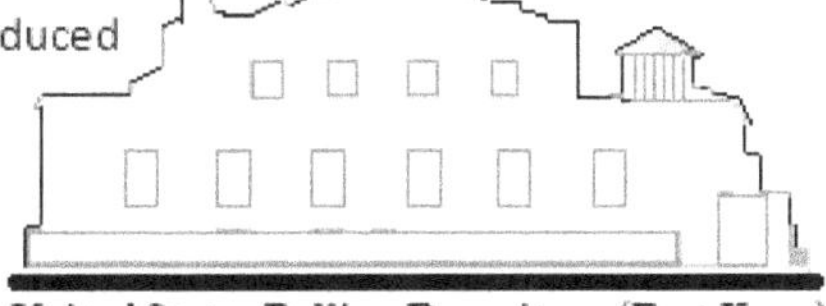
United States Bullion Depository (Fort Knox)

Louisiana

State Name:	Louisiana
Capital:	Baton Rouge
Abbreviations:	LA, La.
Nickname:	The Pelican State
Other Names:	Bayou State; Child of the Mississippi; Creole State; Sportsman's Paradise; Sugar State; The Boot
Motto:	Union, justice, and confidence
Statehood:	April 30, 1812 (18th)
Demonym:	Louisianan
Time Zone:	Central Standard Time
Region/Div:	South / West South Central
Slogan:	Sportsman's Paradise ; Bayou State; LoUiSiAna
Song:	"Give Me Louisiana"
Name Origin:	Named after Louis XIV of France
Brief History:	The first permanent settlement, Fort Maurepas, was founded in 1699 by Pierre Le Moyne d'Iberville, a French military officer. The settlement of Natchitoches was established in 1714 by Louis Juchereau de St. Denis, making it the oldest permanent European settlement in the state of Louisiana. France ceded most of its territory to the east of the Mississippi to Great Britain in 1763, after Britain's victory in the Seven Years' War. In 1762, the rest of Louisiana become a colony of Spain by the Treaty of Fontainebleau. In 1800, France's Napoleon Bonaparte reacquired Louisiana from Spain in the Treaty of San Ildefonso. In 1803, Louisiana became part of the United States through the Louisiana Purchase.

Flag

Seal

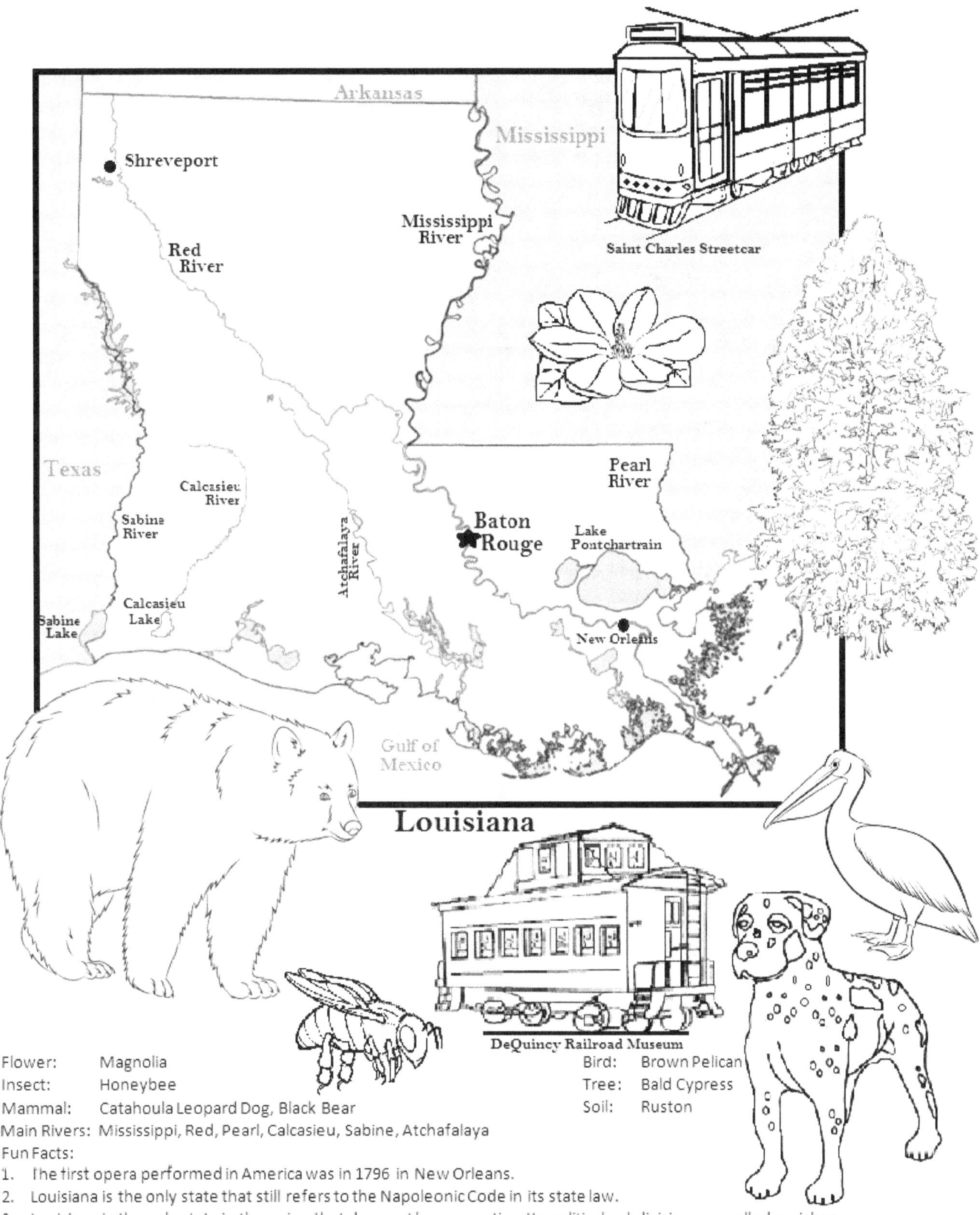

Flower: Magnolia
Insect: Honeybee
Mammal: Catahoula Leopard Dog, Black Bear

Bird: Brown Pelican
Tree: Bald Cypress
Soil: Ruston

Main Rivers: Mississippi, Red, Pearl, Calcasieu, Sabine, Atchafalaya

Fun Facts:

1. The first opera performed in America was in 1796 in New Orleans.
2. Louisiana is the only state that still refers to the Napoleonic Code in its state law.
3. Louisiana is the only state in the union that does not have counties. Its political subdivisions are called parishes.
4. The Saint Charles streetcar line in New Orleans is one of two of the nation's only mobile national monuments.
5. The world famous "Mardi Gras" is celebrated in New Orleans. Mardi Gras colors are Purple (Justice), Gold (Power), and Green (Faith).

Maine

State Name:	Maine
Capital:	Augusta
Abbreviations:	ME; Me.
Nickname:	The Pine Tree State
Other Names:	Vacationland
Motto:	I lead
Statehood:	March 15, 1820 (23rd)
Demonym:	Mainer
Time Zone:	Eastern Standard Time
Region/Div:	Northeast / New England
Slogan:	Vacationland; It Must Be Maine; The Way Life Should Be
Song:	"State Song of Maine"
Name Origin:	The name Maine was chosen by Sir Ferdinando Gorges in 1622 to honor the village where his ancestors first lived in England.
Brief History:	The first European settlement in Maine was in 1604 on Saint Croix Island. The French named the entire area Acadia. The first English settlement in Maine was the Popham Colony in 1607. The coastal areas of western Maine became the Province of Maine in a 1622 land patent. The eastern part of Maine was known as the Territory of Sagadahock. The province within its current boundaries became part of Massachusetts Bay Colony in 1652. The final border was not established until the Webster–Ashburton Treaty of 1842. Under the Missouri Compromise, it was admitted to the Union as the 23rd state.

Flag

Seal

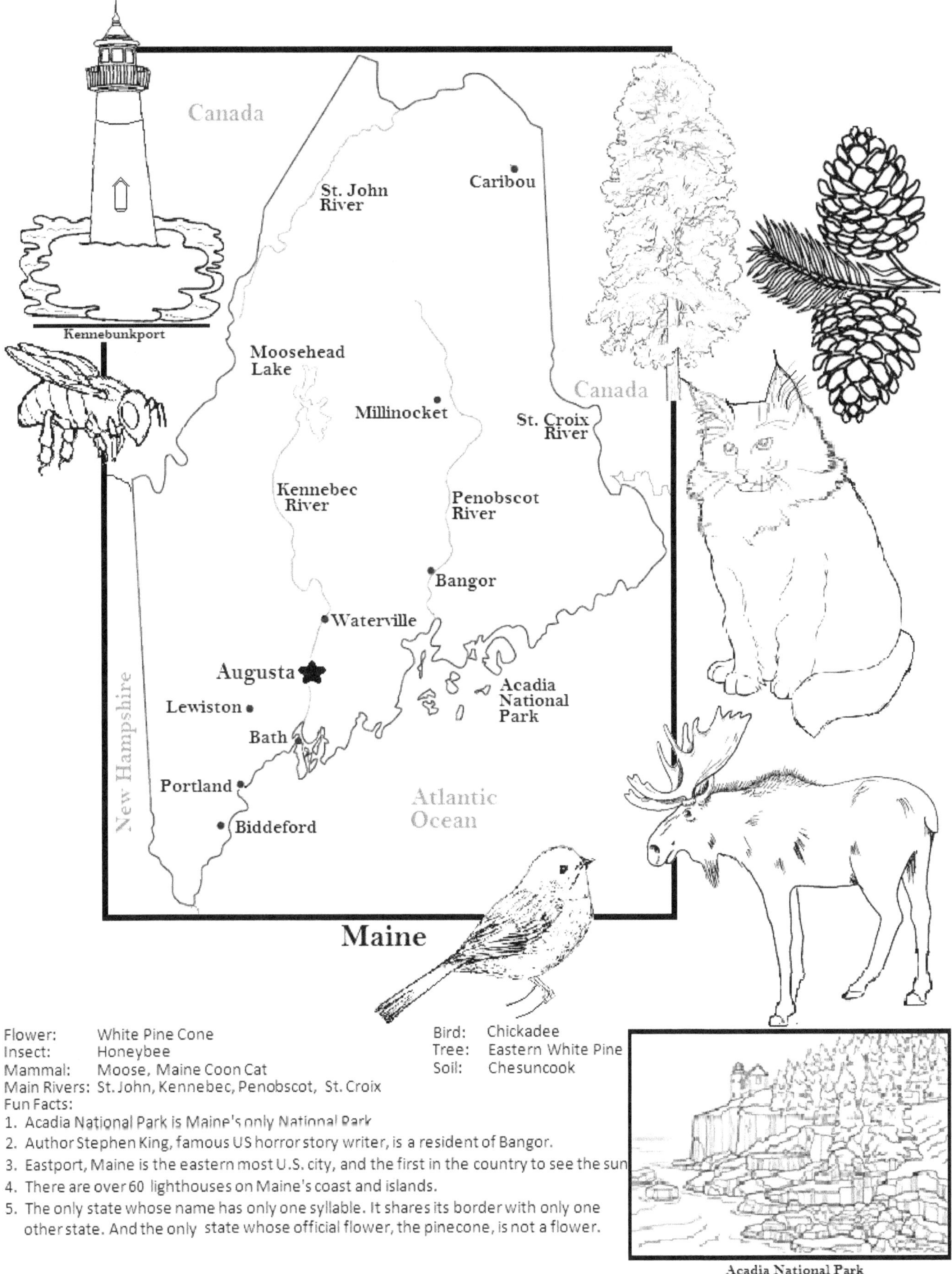

Flower: White Pine Cone
Insect: Honeybee
Mammal: Moose, Maine Coon Cat
Main Rivers: St. John, Kennebec, Penobscot, St. Croix

Bird: Chickadee
Tree: Eastern White Pine
Soil: Chesuncook

Fun Facts:

1. Acadia National Park is Maine's only National Park

2. Author Stephen King, famous US horror story writer, is a resident of Bangor.

3. Eastport, Maine is the eastern most U.S. city, and the first in the country to see the sun

4. There are over 60 lighthouses on Maine's coast and islands.

5. The only state whose name has only one syllable. It shares its border with only one other state. And the only state whose official flower, the pinecone, is not a flower.

Acadia National Park

Maryland

State Name:	Maryland
Capital:	Annapolis
Abbreviations:	MD; Md.
Nickname:	The Old Line State
Other Names:	Free State; Little America; America in Miniature
Motto:	Strong deeds, gentle words
Statehood:	April 28, 1788 (7th)
Demonym:	Marylander
Time Zone:	Eastern Standard Time
Region/Div:	South / South Atlantic
Slogan:	If you're looking for a merry land, go to Maryland!; Drive Carefully; Maryland of Opportunity
Song:	"Maryland! My Maryland!"
Name Origin:	Named after Queen Henrietta Maria of England.
Brief History:	Maryland was one of the thirteen colonies that revolted against the British rule. In 1776, Maryland joined the other American colonies in declaring their independence from Britain. On February 2, 1781, Maryland became the last and 13th state to approve the ratification of the Articles of Confederation and Perpetual Union, first proposed in 1776 and adopted by the Second Continental Congress in 1778, which brought into being the United States as a united, sovereign and national state. In December 1790, Maryland donated land selected by President George Washington to the federal government for the creation of the new national capital of Washington, D.C.

Flag

Seal

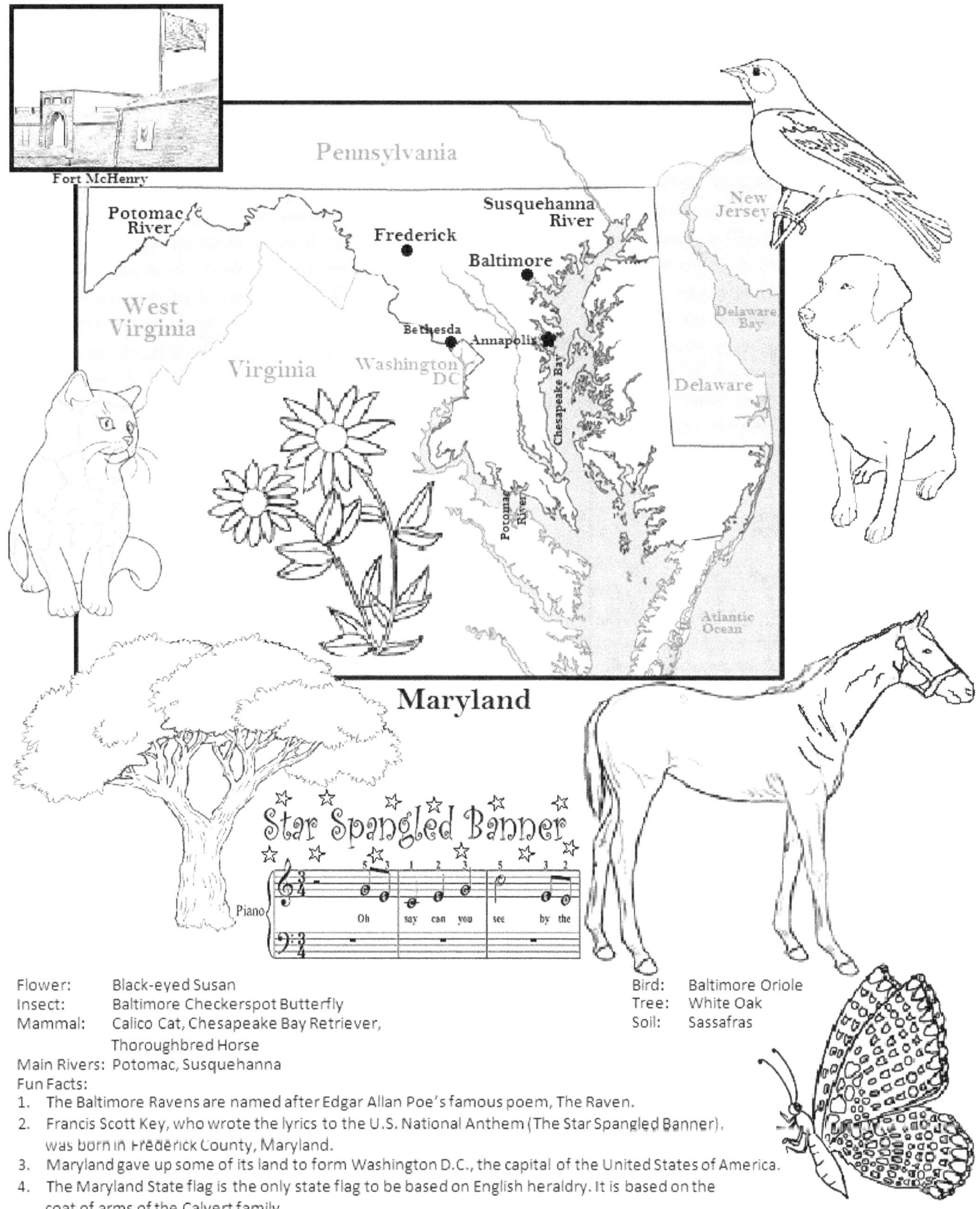

Flower: Black-eyed Susan
Insect: Baltimore Checkerspot Butterfly
Mammal: Calico Cat, Chesapeake Bay Retriever,
               Thoroughbred Horse

Bird: Baltimore Oriole
Tree: White Oak
Soil: Sassafras

Main Rivers: Potomac, Susquehanna

Fun Facts:

1. The Baltimore Ravens are named after Edgar Allan Poe's famous poem, The Raven.
2. Francis Scott Key, who wrote the lyrics to the U.S. National Anthem (The Star Spangled Banner), was born in Frederick County, Maryland.
3. Maryland gave up some of its land to form Washington D.C., the capital of the United States of America.
4. The Maryland State flag is the only state flag to be based on English heraldry. It is based on the coat of arms of the Calvert family.
5. The Susquehanna River at 464 miles long (747 km) is the largest non-navigable river in North America. It is the longest river on the East Coast of the United States that drains into the Atlantic Ocean and the longest river in the United States without commercial boat traffic.

Massachusetts

State Name:	Commonwealth of Massachusetts
Capital:	Boston
Abbreviations:	MA; Mass.
Nickname:	The Bay State
Other Names:	The Pilgrim State; The Puritan State; The Old Colony State; The Baked Bean State
Motto:	By the sword we seek peace, but peace only under liberty
Statehood:	February 6, 1788 (6th)
Demonym:	Massachusettsan
Time Zone:	Eastern Standard Time
Region/Div:	Northeast / New England
Slogan:	The Spirit of America
Song:	"All Hail to Massachusetts"
Name Origin:	From Algonquian Massachusett, meaning "at the large hill, in reference to the Great Blue Hill, southwest of Boston. A name for the native people who lived around the bay.
Brief History:	In 1620 the Pilgrims landed in Plymouth Massachusetts via the Mayflower and set up a settlement. The event known as the "First Thanksgiving" was celebrated by the Pilgrims after their first harvest in the New World. Massachusetts was one of the Thirteen Colonies that revolted against British rule in the American Revolution and one of the original 13 colonies that would eventually form the United States of America.

Flag

Seal

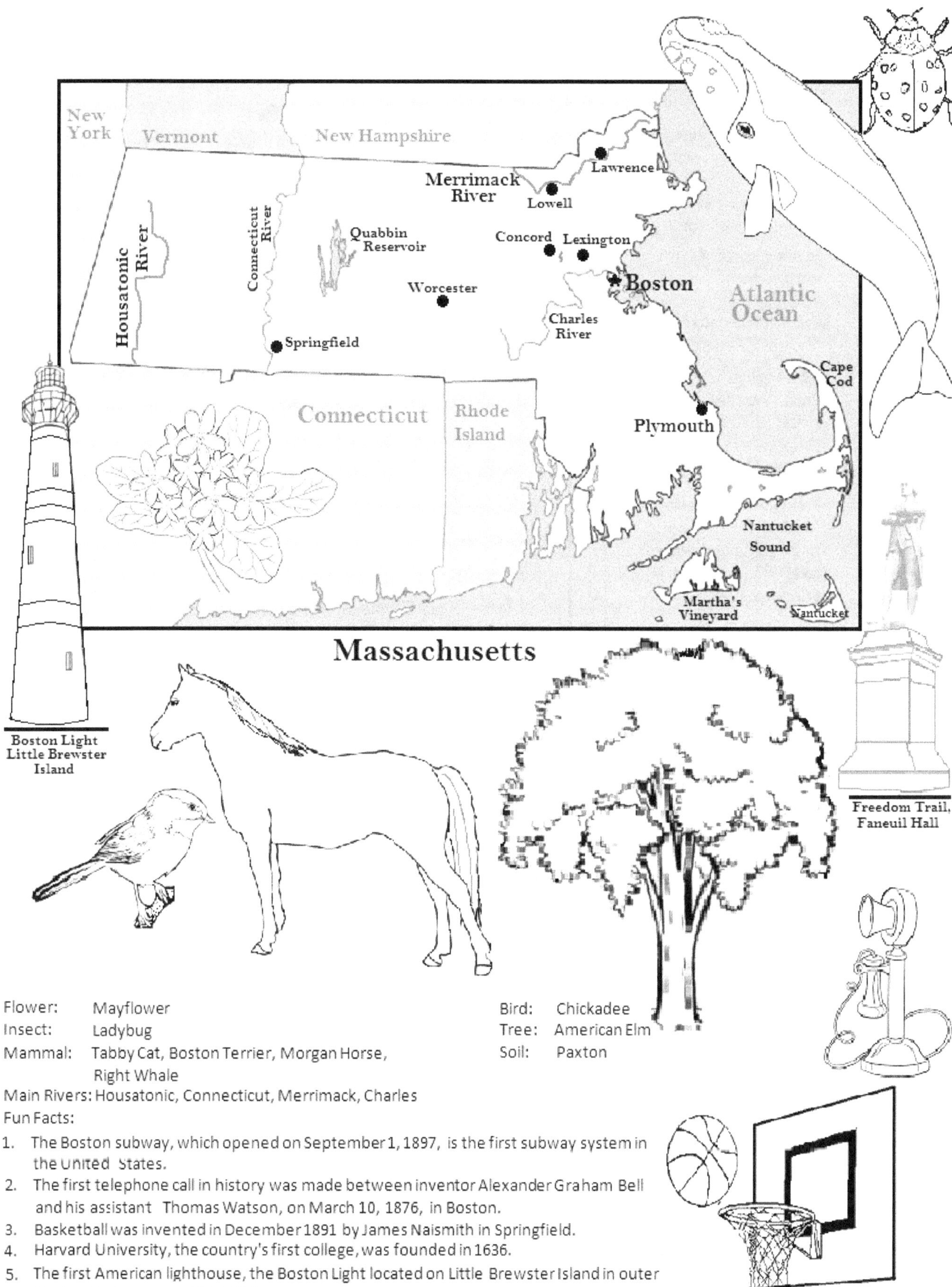

Massachusetts

Flower: Mayflower
Insect: Ladybug
Mammal: Tabby Cat, Boston Terrier, Morgan Horse, Right Whale

Bird: Chickadee
Tree: American Elm
Soil: Paxton

Main Rivers: Housatonic, Connecticut, Merrimack, Charles

Fun Facts:

1. The Boston subway, which opened on September 1, 1897, is the first subway system in the United States.
2. The first telephone call in history was made between inventor Alexander Graham Bell and his assistant Thomas Watson, on March 10, 1876, in Boston.
3. Basketball was invented in December 1891 by James Naismith in Springfield.
4. Harvard University, the country's first college, was founded in 1636.
5. The first American lighthouse, the Boston Light located on Little Brewster Island in outer Boston Harbor was built in 1716.

Michigan

State Name:	Michigan
Capital:	Lansing
Abbreviations:	MI; Mich.
Nickname:	The Wolverine State
Other Names:	The Great Lakes State and Water Winter Wonderland
Motto:	If you seek a pleasant peninsula, look about you
Statehood:	January 26, 1837 (26th)
Demonym:	Michiganian
Time Zone:	Eastern Standard Time
Region/Div:	Midwest / East North Central
Slogan:	Pure Michigan; Water Wonderland; Water Winter Wonderland; Great Lakes State;
Song:	Michigan, My Michigan
Name Origin:	From a French spelling of Old Ojibwa (Algonquian) mishi-gamaa, meaning "big lake." referring to Lake Michigan
Brief History:	The first permanent European settlement was founded in 1668 by the French. In 1763, the British gained control of Michigan after winning the French and Indian War. Under the 1763 Treaty of Paris, Michigan and the rest of New France east of the Mississippi River passed to Great Britain. In 1787, Michigan became part of the Northwest Territory of the United States. Michigan once again was taken over by the British at the start of the War of 1812. The Americans tried to take back Detroit at the Battle of Frenchtown in January of 1813, but were defeated. But later that year the Americans defeated the British at the Battle of Lake Erie and took back Detroit.

Flag

Seal

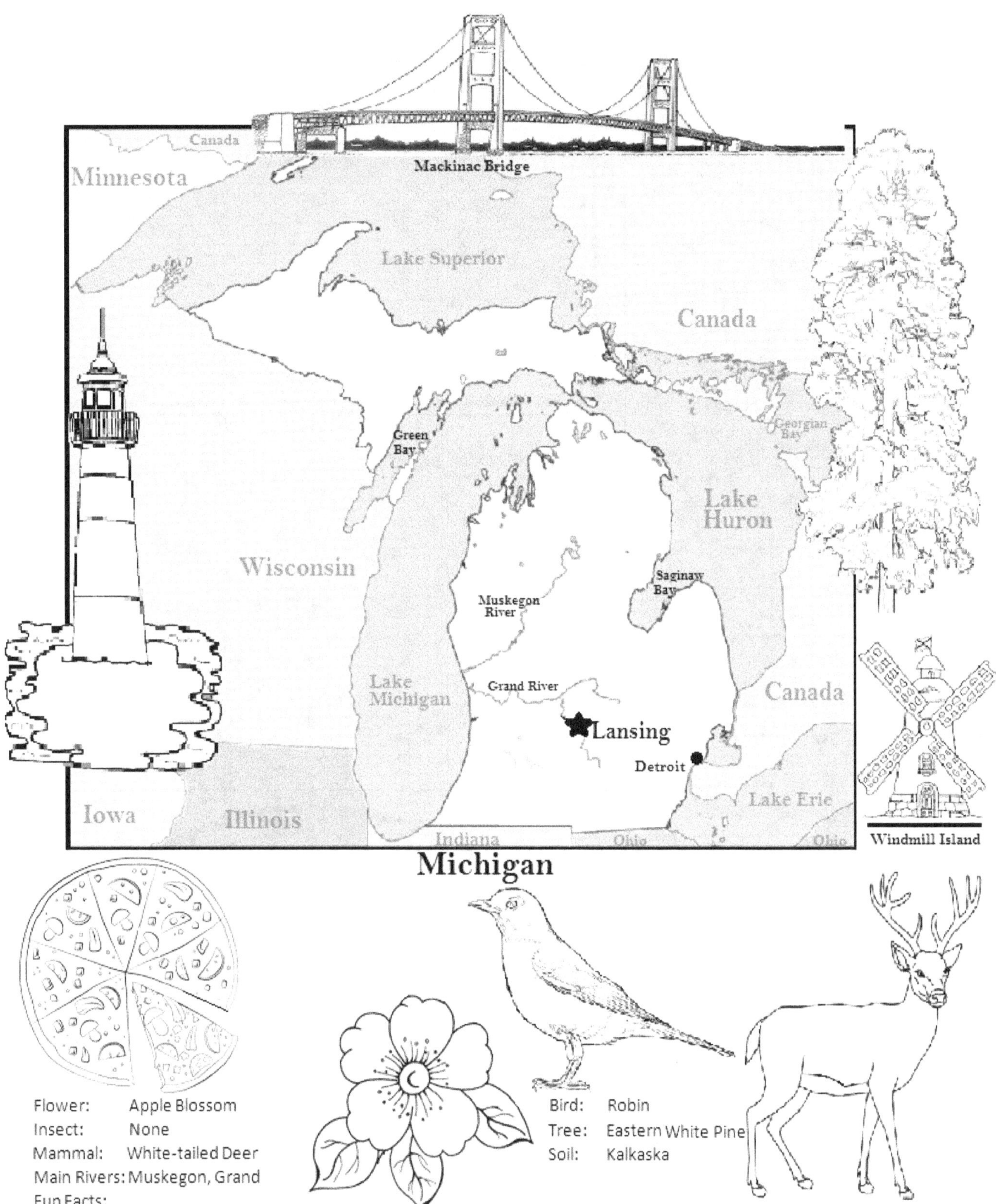

Michigan

Flower: Apple Blossom	Bird: Robin
Insect: None	Tree: Eastern White Pine
Mammal: White-tailed Deer	Soil: Kalkaska
Main Rivers: Muskegon, Grand	

Fun Facts:

1. With 150 functioning and non-functioning lighthouses, Michigan has more lighthouses than any other state.
2. One of the longest suspension bridges in the world is called the Mackinac Bridge and it connects Michigan's upper and lower peninsulas.
3. With approximately 3,288 miles of coastline, Michigan boasts the longest freshwater coastline in the world.
4. Michigan is the only state consisting of two peninsulas, upper and lower.
5. Two of the top four pizza chains were founded and are headquartered in this state: Domino's Pizza and Little Caesars Pizza.

Minnesota

State Name:	Minnesota
Capital:	St. Paul
Abbreviations:	MN; Minn.
Nickname:	The North Star State
Other Names:	Land of 10,000 Lakes; The Wheat State; The Bread and Butter State; The Gopher State
Motto:	The star of the north
Statehood:	May 11, 1858 (32nd)
Demonym:	Minnesotan
Time Zone:	Central Standard Time
Region/Div:	Midwest / West North Central
Slogan:	Land of 10,000 lakes; Explore
Song:	"Hail Minnesota"
Name Origin:	Named for the river, from Dakota Indian name mnisota, meaning "cloudy water, milky water"

Brief History: In 1762 the region became part of Spanish Louisiana until 1802. In 1803, The United States acquired the western portion of the area through the Louisiana Purchase. In 1805, The U.S. purchased land for Fort Snelling. The northern part of Minnesota was ceded by the British on 1818. The area of Minnesota became part of Michigan Territory from 1818 until 1836 when it became part of Wisconsin Territory. On March 3 1849, the US Congress created the Minnesota Territory.

Flag

Seal

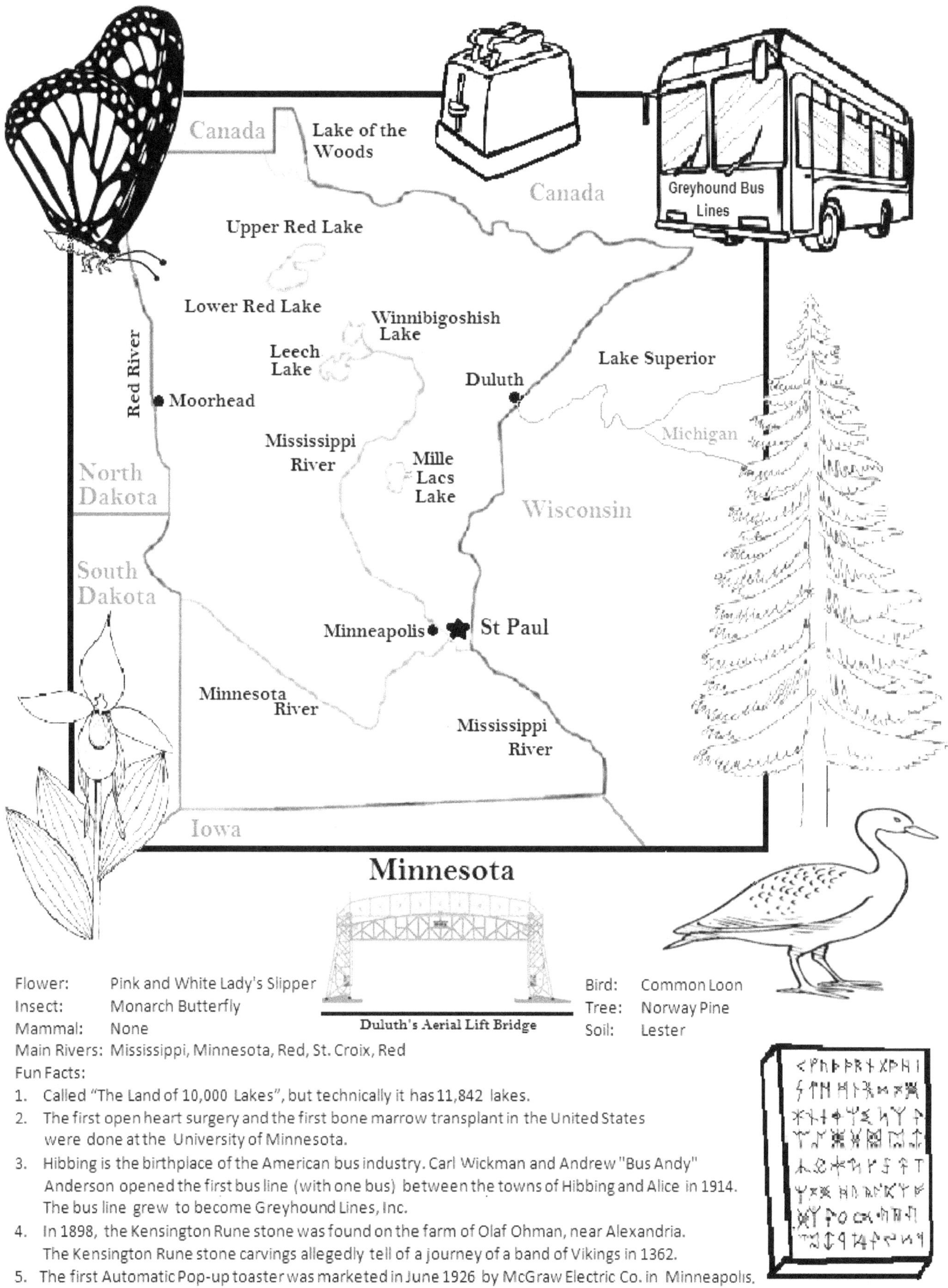

Minnesota

Flower: Pink and White Lady's Slipper
Insect: Monarch Butterfly
Mammal: None

Bird: Common Loon
Tree: Norway Pine
Soil: Lester

Main Rivers: Mississippi, Minnesota, Red, St. Croix, Red

Fun Facts:

1. Called "The Land of 10,000 Lakes", but technically it has 11,842 lakes.
2. The first open heart surgery and the first bone marrow transplant in the United States were done at the University of Minnesota.
3. Hibbing is the birthplace of the American bus industry. Carl Wickman and Andrew "Bus Andy" Anderson opened the first bus line (with one bus) between the towns of Hibbing and Alice in 1914. The bus line grew to become Greyhound Lines, Inc.
4. In 1898, the Kensington Rune stone was found on the farm of Olaf Ohman, near Alexandria. The Kensington Rune stone carvings allegedly tell of a journey of a band of Vikings in 1362.
5. The first Automatic Pop-up toaster was marketed in June 1926 by McGraw Electric Co. in Minneapolis, under the name Toastmaster.

Kensington Rune

Mississippi

State Name:	Mississippi
Capital:	Jackson
Abbreviations:	MS; Miss.
Nickname:	The Magnolia State
Other Names:	The Hospitality State; Eagle State; Groundhog State
Motto:	By valor and arms
Statehood:	December 10, 1817 (20th)
Demonym:	Mississippian
Time Zone:	Central Standard Time
Region/Div:	South / East South Central
Slogan:	The Hospitality State; Feels Like Coming Home; The South's Warmest Welcome; The Magnolia State
Song:	"Go, Mississippi"
Name Origin:	From French variation of Algonquian Ojibwa meshi-ziibi, meaning "big river."
Brief History:	In 1699, the French colonists established the first European settlement at Fort Maurepas (also known as Old Biloxi). Through the 18th century, the area was ruled variously by Spanish, French, and British colonial governments. After the American Revolution (1765–83), Britain ceded this area to the new United States of America. On April 7, 1798, Congress organized the Mississippi Territory. Parts of the territory were acquired from Georgia, South Carolina, Spain and from Native American tribes. In 1830, the Choctaw Indians sold part of the Mississippi to the US in the Treaty of Dancing Rabbit Creek.

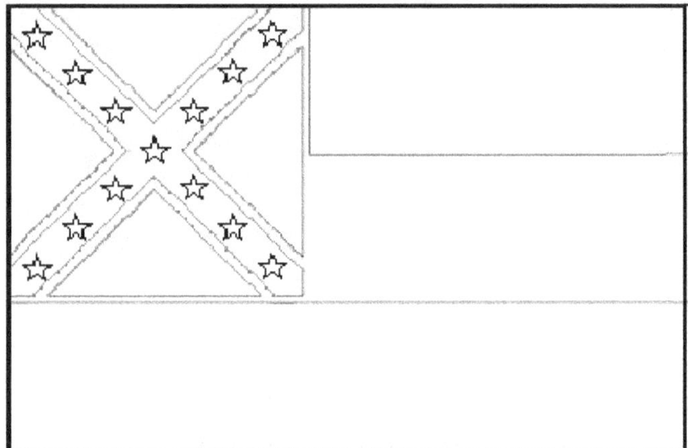

Flag

Seal

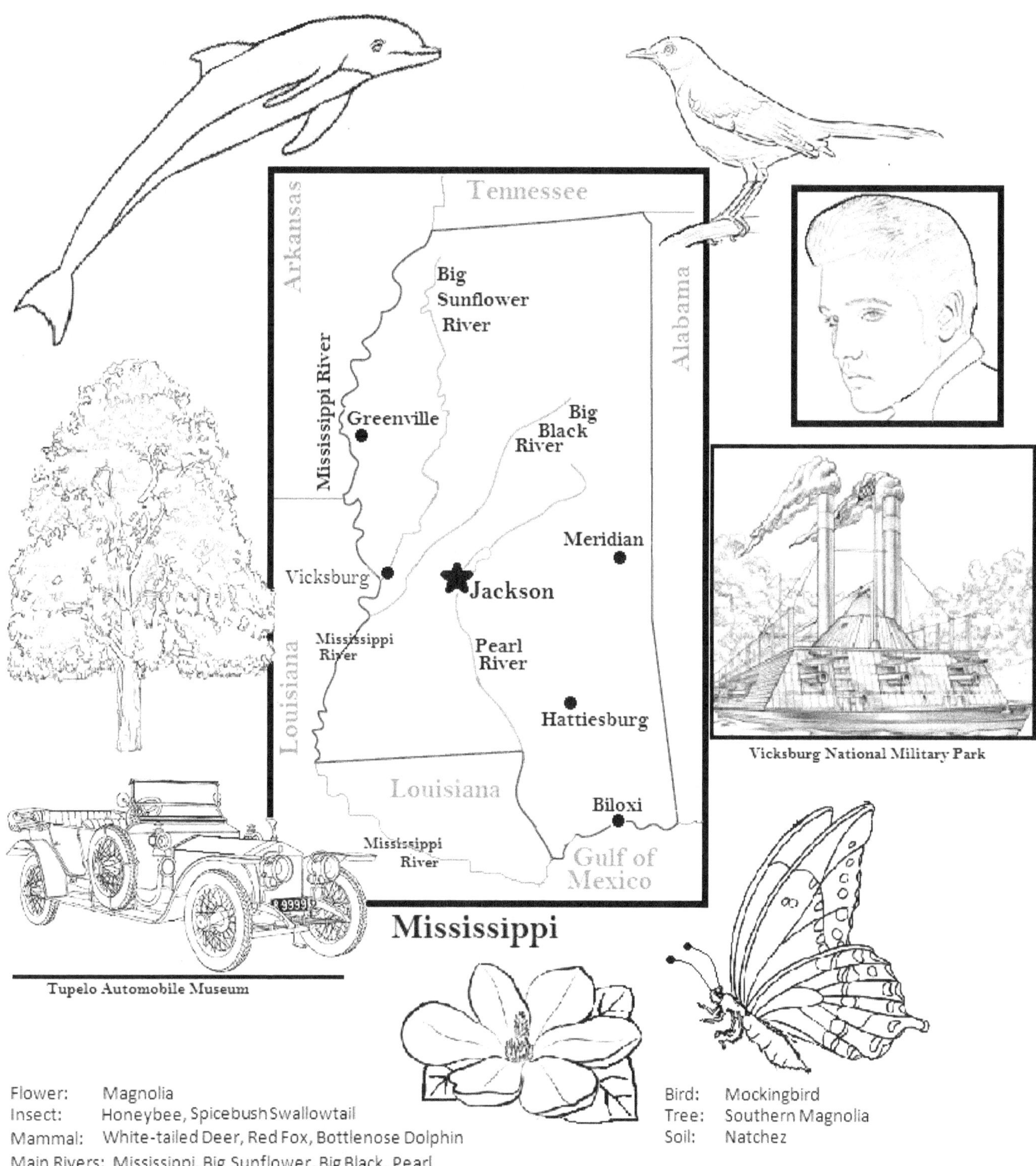

Vicksburg National Military Park

Tupelo Automobile Museum

Flower: Magnolia
Insect: Honeybee, Spicebush Swallowtail
Mammal: White-tailed Deer, Red Fox, Bottlenose Dolphin

Bird: Mockingbird
Tree: Southern Magnolia
Soil: Natchez

Main Rivers: Mississippi, Big Sunflower, Big Black, Pearl

Fun Facts:
1. On January 8, 1935 American icon, Elvis Presley, was born in Tupelo.
2. At 2,320 miles (3,734 km), The Mississippi River (also known as Old Man River) is the longest river in North America.
3. The world's first lung transplant took place in 1963 at the University of Mississippi by Dr. James Hardy and, on January 23, 1964, Hardy performed the world's first heart transplant surgery.
4. In 1902 while on a hunting expedition in Sharkey County, President Theodore (Teddy) Roosevelt refused to shoot a captured bear. This act resulted in the creation of the world-famous teddy bear.
5. When Mississippi cotton planter Isaac Ross died in 1836, his will decreed that his plantation, Prospect Hill, should be liquidated and the proceeds from the sale be used to pay for his slaves' passage to the newly established colony of Liberia in West Africa. It was this group of slaves who founded Liberia.

Missouri

State Name:	Missouri
Capital:	Jefferson City
Abbreviations:	MO; Mo.
Nickname:	The Show-Me State
Other Names:	Gateway to the West;
	The Ozark State;
	The Lead State;
	The Bullion State;
	The Cave State
Motto:	Let the good of the people be the supreme law
Statehood:	August 10, 1821 (24th)
Demonym:	Missourian
Time Zone:	Central Standard Time
Region/Div:	Midwest / West North Central
Slogan:	Show-Me State
Song:	"Missouri Waltz"
Name Origin:	Named for the Missouri River, which was named after the indigenous Missouri Indians, a Siouan- language tribe. It is said that they were called the ouemessourita (wimihsoorita), meaning "town of the large canoes".
Brief History:	During the 1800s, the first European settlers, mostly French Canadians, created their first settlement in Missouri at present-day Ste. Genevieve. In 1762, the Spaniards took over the area from France with the Treaty of Fontainebleau. In 1800, Napoleon Bonaparte took it back from Spain under the Treaty of San Ildefonso. Then, the U.S. acquired the land from France as part of the Louisiana Purchase in 1803. On June 4, 1812, Congress created the Missouri Territory.

Flag

Seal

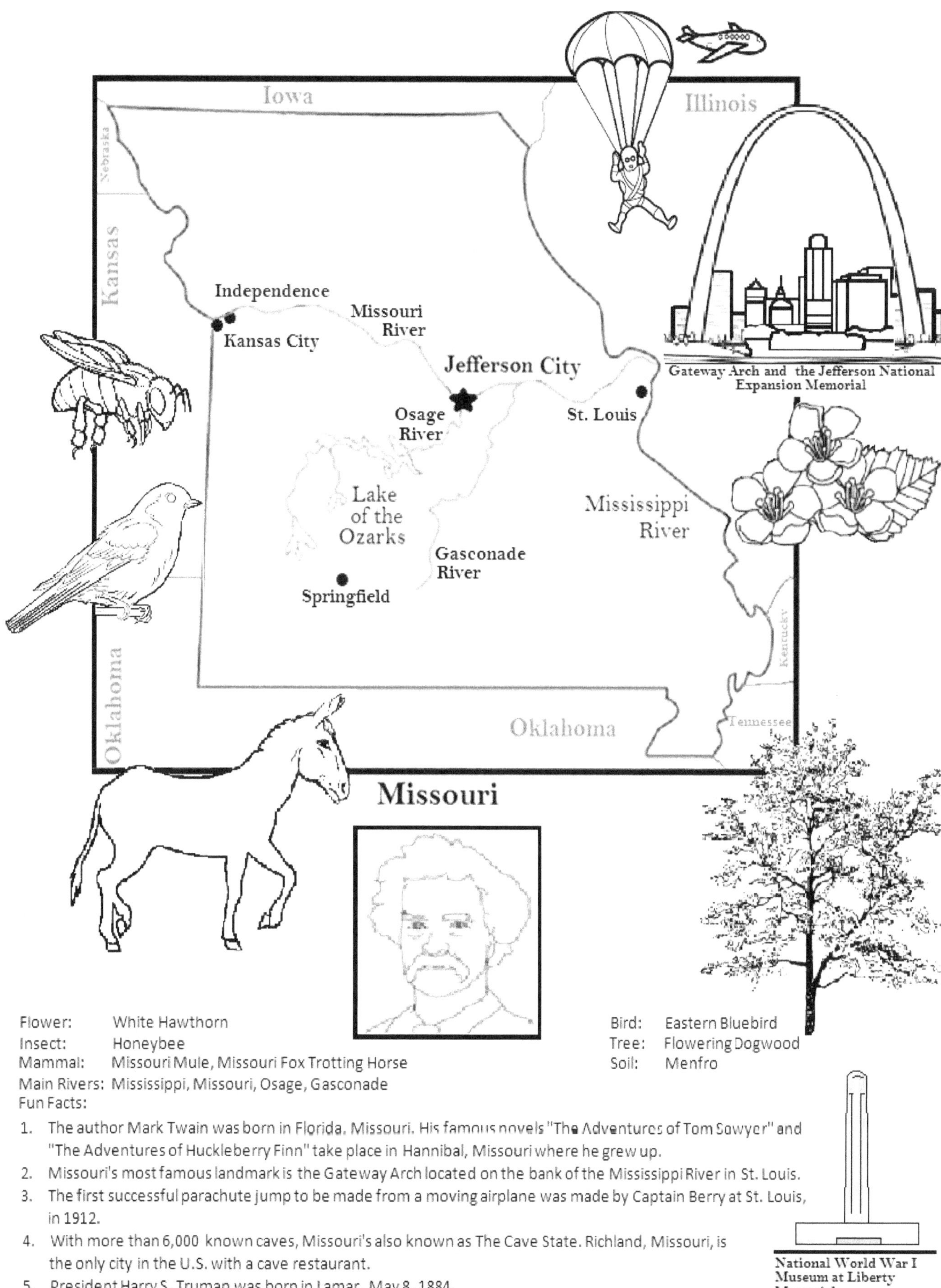

Flower:	White Hawthorn		Bird:	Eastern Bluebird
Insect:	Honeybee		Tree:	Flowering Dogwood
Mammal:	Missouri Mule, Missouri Fox Trotting Horse		Soil:	Menfro

Main Rivers: Mississippi, Missouri, Osage, Gasconade

Fun Facts:

1. The author Mark Twain was born in Florida, Missouri. His famous novels "The Adventures of Tom Sawyer" and "The Adventures of Huckleberry Finn" take place in Hannibal, Missouri where he grew up.
2. Missouri's most famous landmark is the Gateway Arch located on the bank of the Mississippi River in St. Louis.
3. The first successful parachute jump to be made from a moving airplane was made by Captain Berry at St. Louis, in 1912.
4. With more than 6,000 known caves, Missouri's also known as The Cave State. Richland, Missouri, is the only city in the U.S. with a cave restaurant.
5. President Harry S. Truman was born in Lamar, May 8, 1884.

Montana

State Name:	Montana
Capital:	Helena
Abbreviations:	MT; Mont.
Nickname:	The Treasure State
Other Names:	Land of the Shining Mountains; The Last Best Place
Motto:	Gold and silver
Statehood:	November 8, 1889 (41st)
Demonym:	Montanan
Time Zone:	Mountain Standard Time
Region/Div:	West / Mountain
Slogan:	The Treasure State; Big Sky Country
Song:	"Montana"
Name Origin:	From the Spanish word montaña, meaning "mountain". U.S. Rep. James H. Ashley of Ohio proposed the name in 1864.
Brief History:	The first trading post Fort Raymond (1807-1811) was constructed in Crow Indian country in 1807. The first permanent settlement by Euro-Americans in what today is Montana was St. Mary's (1841) near present-day Stevensville. Various parts of what is now Montana became parts of Oregon Territory, Washington Territory, Idaho Territory and Dakota Territory. Prior to the Oregon Treaty (1846), the land west of the continental divide was disputed between the British and U.S. and was known as the Oregon Country. The land in Montana east of the continental divide was part of the Louisiana Purchase in 1803. The Territory of Montana (1864-1889) was an organized incorporated territory of the United States until it was admitted in the union.

Flag

Seal

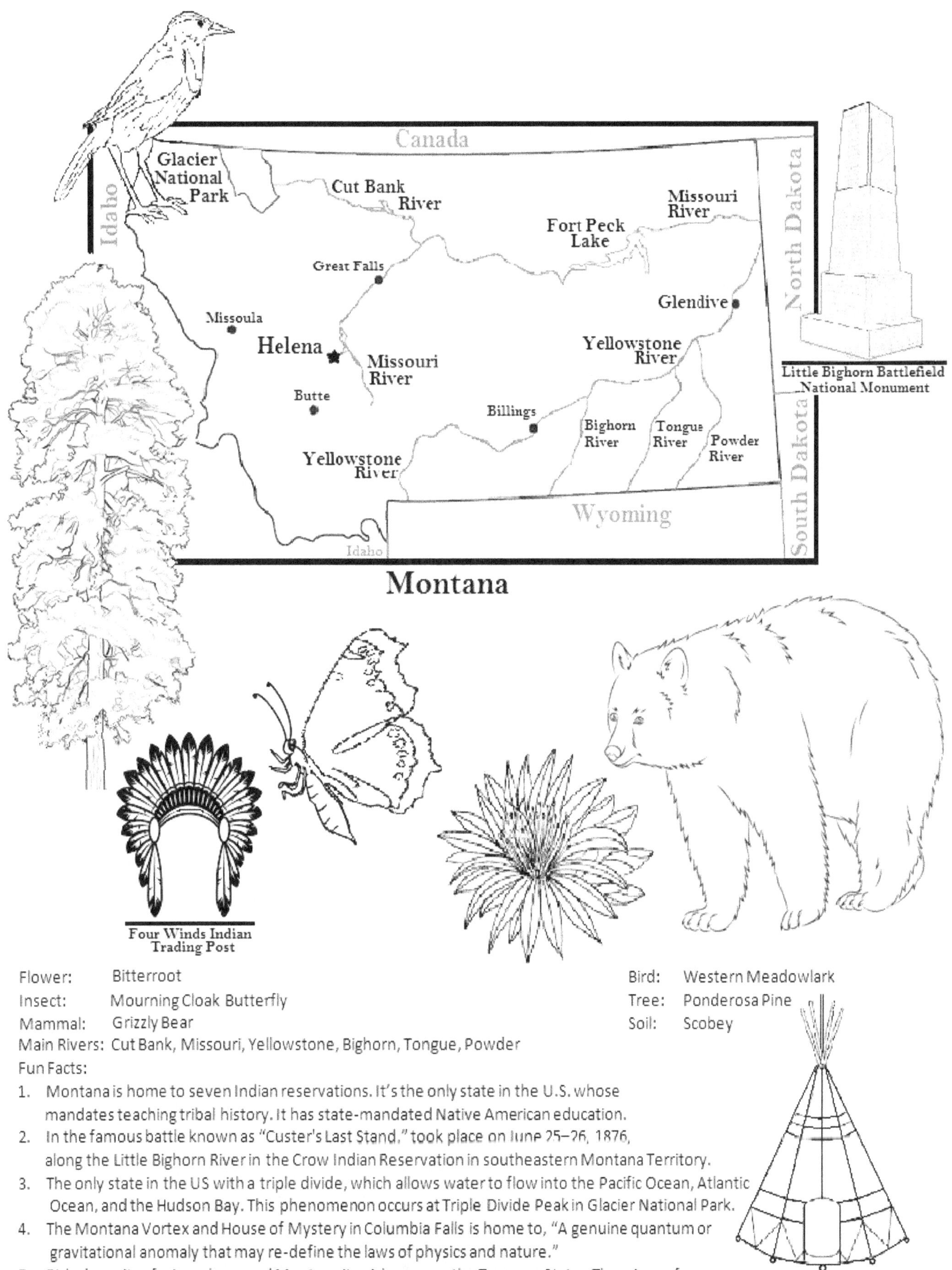

Flower: Bitterroot

Insect: Mourning Cloak Butterfly

Mammal: Grizzly Bear

Bird: Western Meadowlark

Tree: Ponderosa Pine

Soil: Scobey

Main Rivers: Cut Bank, Missouri, Yellowstone, Bighorn, Tongue, Powder

Fun Facts:

1. Montana is home to seven Indian reservations. It's the only state in the U.S. whose mandates teaching tribal history. It has state-mandated Native American education.

2. In the famous battle known as "Custer's Last Stand," took place on June 25–26, 1876, along the Little Bighorn River in the Crow Indian Reservation in southeastern Montana Territory.

3. The only state in the US with a triple divide, which allows water to flow into the Pacific Ocean, Atlantic Ocean, and the Hudson Bay. This phenomenon occurs at Triple Divide Peak in Glacier National Park.

4. The Montana Vortex and House of Mystery in Columbia Falls is home to, "A genuine quantum or gravitational anomaly that may re-define the laws of physics and nature."

5. Rich deposits of minerals earned Montana its nickname as the Treasure State. The mines of Montana made Helena home to more millionaires, per capita, than any other city in the world.

Nebraska

State Name:	Nebraska
Capital:	Lincoln
Abbreviations:	NE; Neb.
Nickname:	The Cornhusker State
Other Names:	The Heart of Dixie; The Cotton State; Plantation State; The Lizard State
Motto:	Equality before the law
Statehood:	March 1, 1867 (37th)
Demonym:	Nebraskan
Time Zone:	Central Standard Time ; Mountain Standard Time
Region/Div:	Midwest / West North Central
Slogan:	The Beef State; Cornhusker State
Song:	"Beautiful Nebraska"
Name Origin:	Based on an Oto Indian word Nebrathka meaning "flat water" (referring to the Platte River, which is also an official symbol of Nebraska).
Brief History:	In 1541, Spanish explorer Francisco Vasquez de Coronado claimed the entire territory for Spain. In 1682 French explorer Rene Cavalier, claimed all the land Robert drained by the Mississippi for France. The land that included Nebraska, was named "Louisiana" in honor of French King Louis XIV. In 1720, a Spanish expedition went to Nebraska to remove the French. But the Pawnee Indians attacked and killed most of the Spaniards. In 1800, French ruler Napoleon Bonaparte forced Spain to return the Louisiana Territory to France and sold the entire territory, which included Nebraska, to the United States in 1803. This transaction is known as the Louisiana Purchase.

Flag

Seal

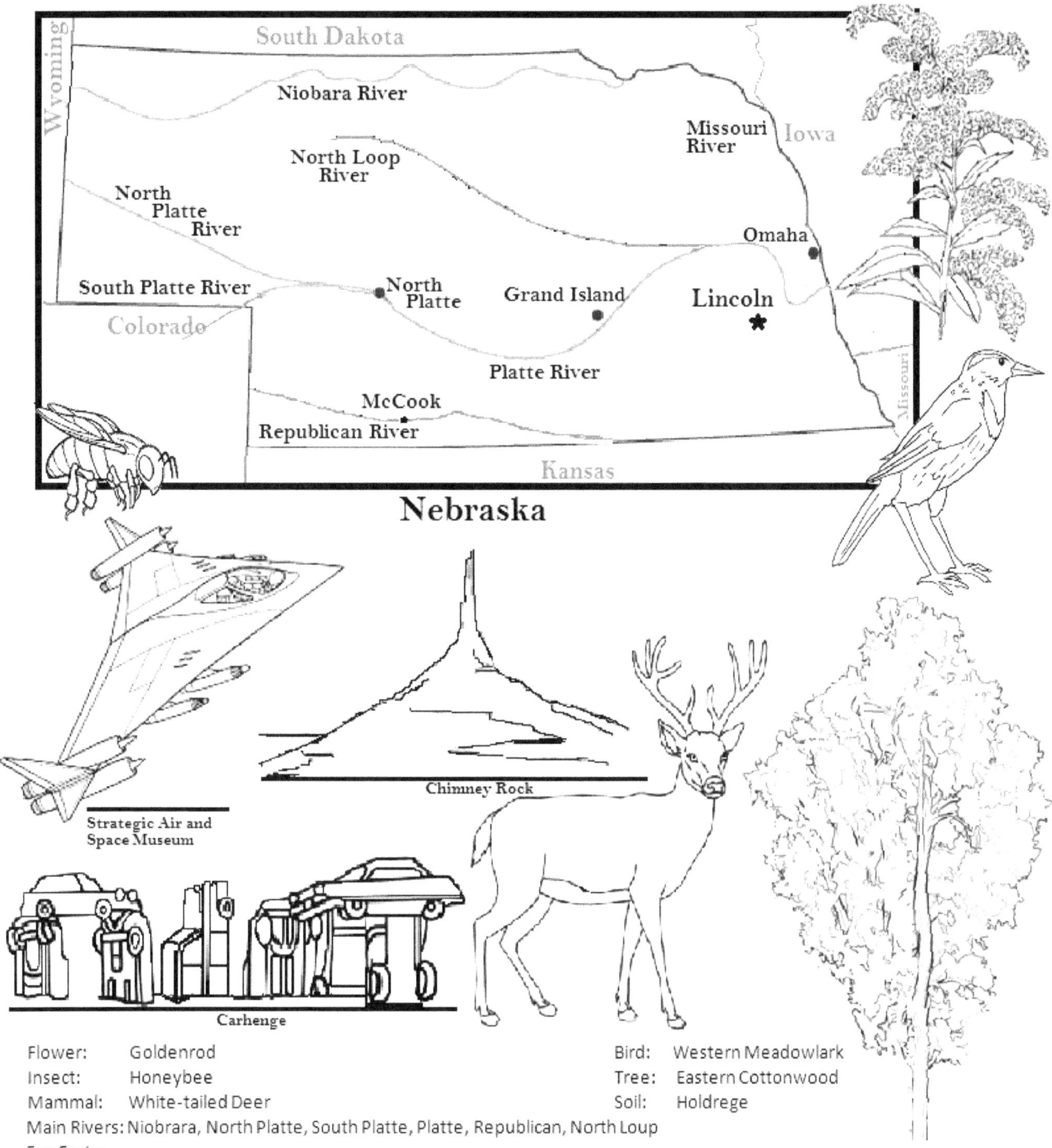

Flower:	Goldenrod	Bird:	Western Meadowlark
Insect:	Honeybee	Tree:	Eastern Cottonwood
Mammal:	White-tailed Deer	Soil:	Holdrege

Main Rivers: Niobrara, North Platte, South Platte, Platte, Republican, North Loup

Fun Facts:

1. The Henry Doorly Zoo in Omaha, Nebraska, houses the largest indoor rainforest in the United States. The Lied Jungle, covering 1.5 acres of land features flora, fauna and animals from rainforests all over the globe.

2. Chimney Rock, a prominent geological rock formation rising nearly 300 feet above the surrounding North Platte River valley, served as a landmark along the Oregon Trail, the California Trail, and the Mormon Trail during the mid-19th century.

3. Nebraska is the only state in the union with a unicameral (one house) legislature.

4. The Carhenge, a replica of the historic English Stonehenge, is located just north of Alliance, Nebraska and is made up of 38 old automobiles that have been arranged similarly to the original Stonehenge.

5. Nebraska is where "Arbor Day" first began in 1872. In 1885 Arbor Day became a legal holiday in Nebraska and it was moved to April 22, the birthday of its founder Julius Sterling Morton.

Nevada

State Name:	Nevada
Capital:	Carson City
Abbreviations:	NV, Nev.
Nickname:	The Silver State
Other Names:	Sagebrush State; Silver State; Battle-Born State; Divorce State
Motto:	All for Our Country and Battle Born
Statehood:	October 31, 1864 (36th)
Demonym:	Nevadan
Time Zone:	Pacific Standard Time; Jackpot and West Wendover: Mountain Standard Time
Region/Div:	West / Mountain
Slogan:	The Silver State
Song:	"Home Means Nevada"
Name Origin:	From the Spanish "Sierra Nevada" (which is also a mountain range in Spain), meaning snow-covered mountain range.
Brief History:	Nevada was part of the area ceded by Mexico to the United States after the Mexican War (1847-1848). When Utah Territory was organized in 1850, almost all of present-day Nevada was included except the southern part, which became part of the New Mexico Territory. On March 2, 1861, Congress created the Nevada Territory.

Flag

Seal

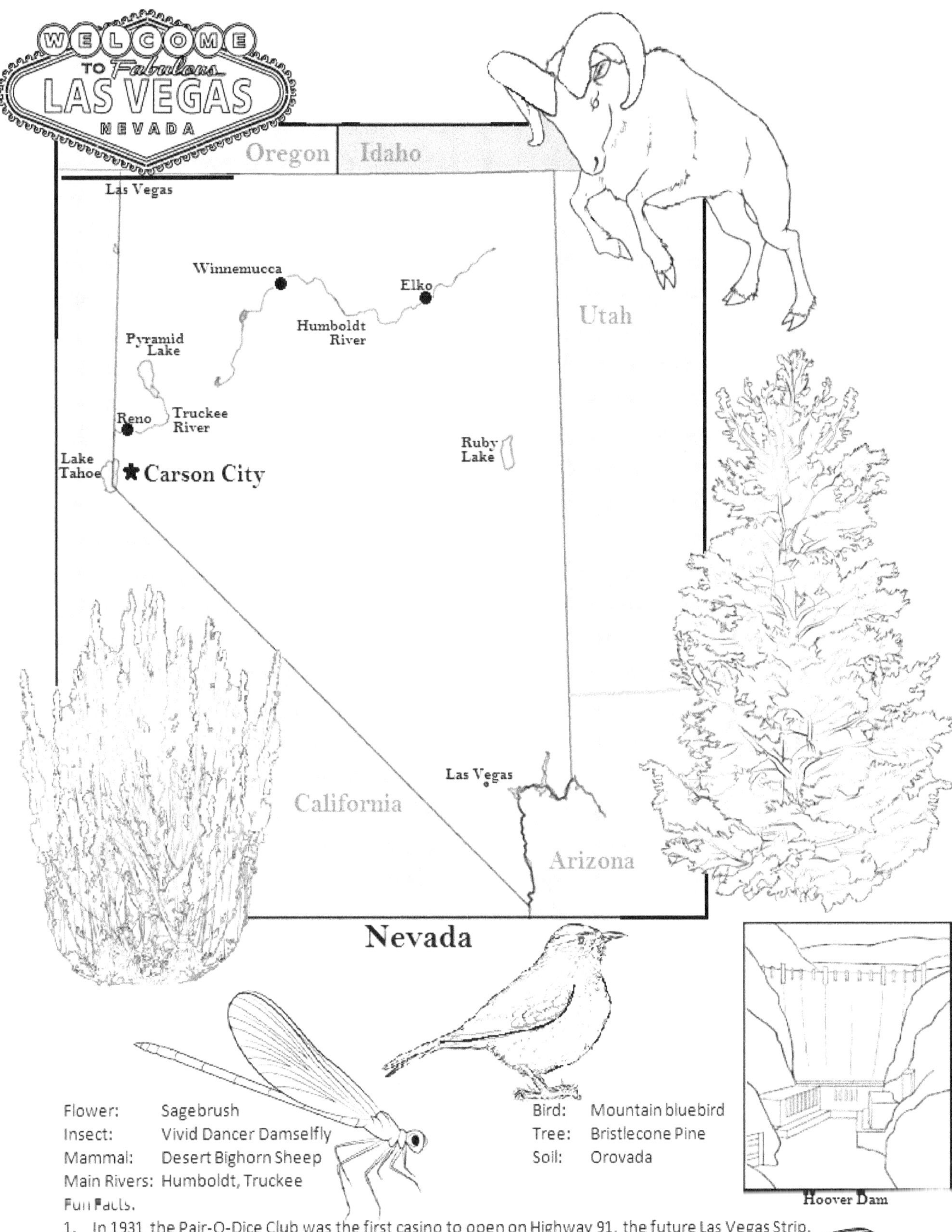

Flower: Sagebrush
Insect: Vivid Dancer Damselfly
Mammal: Desert Bighorn Sheep
Main Rivers: Humboldt, Truckee

Bird: Mountain bluebird
Tree: Bristlecone Pine
Soil: Orovada

Fun Facts:

1. In 1931 the Pair-O-Dice Club was the first casino to open on Highway 91, the future Las Vegas Strip.
2. In Death Valley, the Kangaroo Rat can live its entire life without drinking a drop of liquid.
3. The longest morse code telegram ever sent was the Nevada state constitution. Sent from Carson City to Washington D.C. in 1864.
4. In 1931, the state created two industries, divorce, and gambling. For many years, Reno and Las Vegas were the "divorce capitals of the nation."
5. Construction worker Hard Hat's were first invented specifically for workers on the Hoover Dam in 1933.

New Hampshire

State Name:	New Hampshire
Capital:	Concord
Abbreviations:	NH; N.H.
Nickname:	The Granite State
Other Name:	White Mountain State
Motto:	Live Free or Die
Statehood:	June 21, 1788 (9th)
Demonym:	New Hampshirite
Time Zone:	Eastern Standard Time
Region/Div:	Northeast / New England
Slogan:	Scenic; Photoscenic; First for Independence
Song:	"Old New Hampshire"
Name Origin:	Named by Captain John Mason after Hampshire, England
Brief History:	In January 1776, it became the first of the British North American colonies to establish a government independent from Great Britain. New Hampshire was one of the thirteen colonies that rebelled against the British rule during the American Revolution

Flag

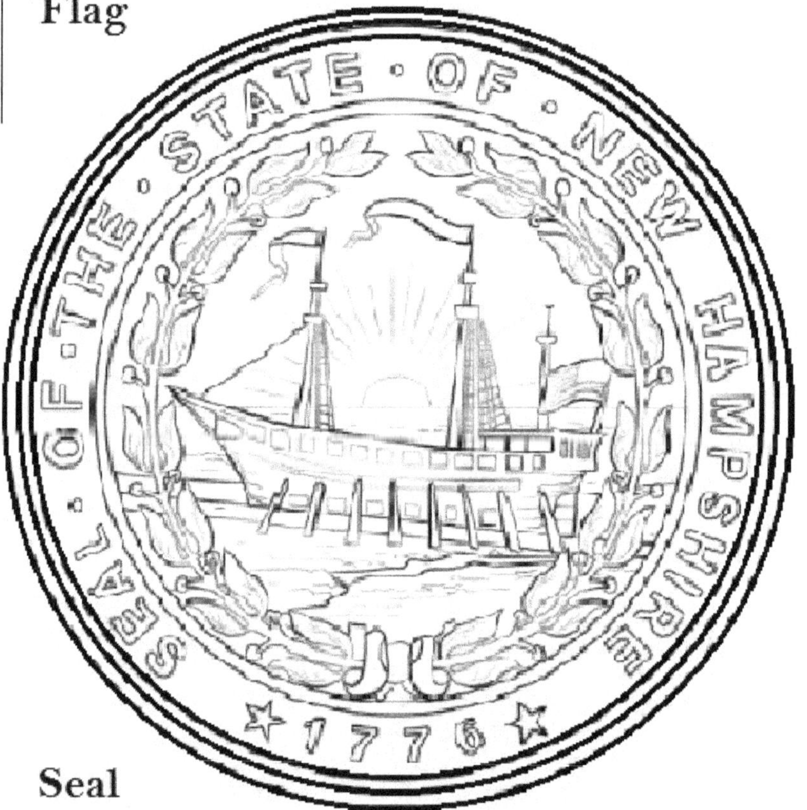

Seal

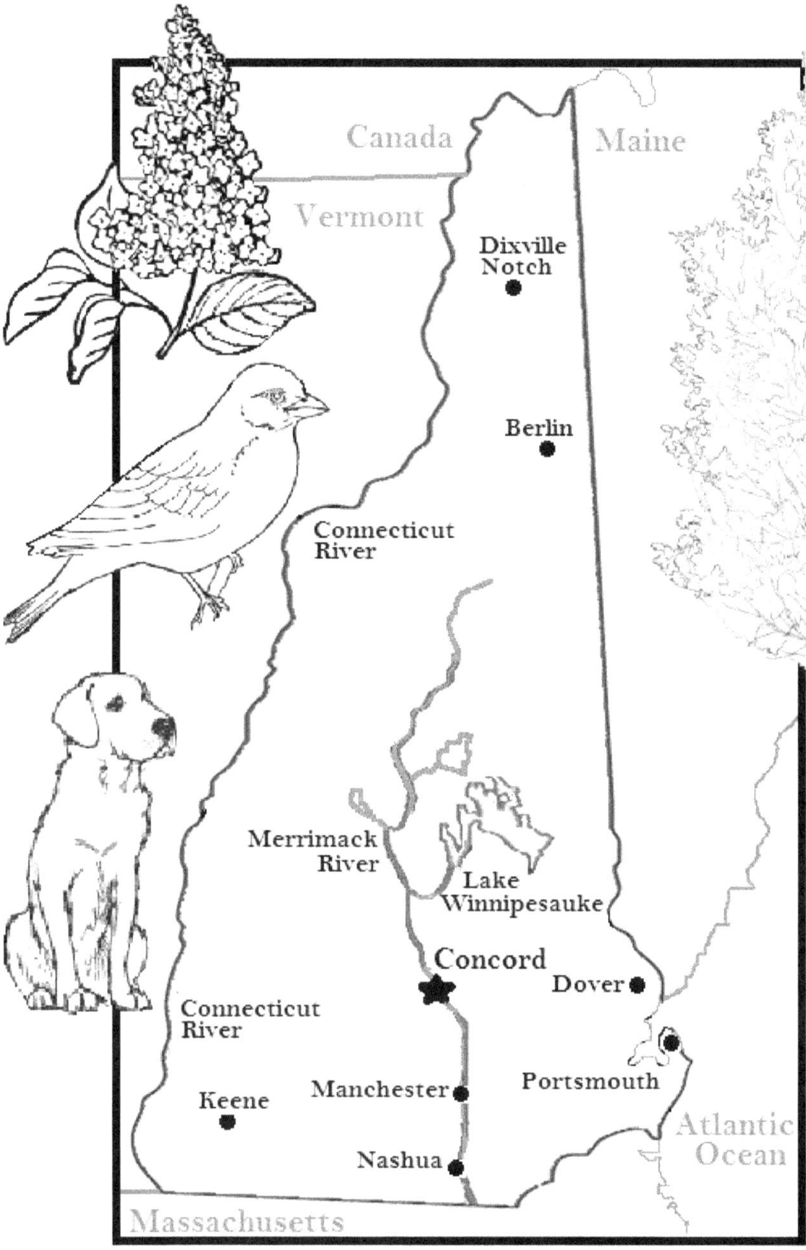

New Hampshire

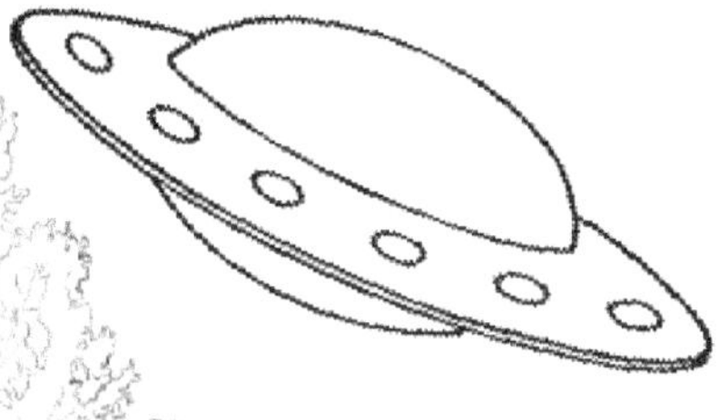

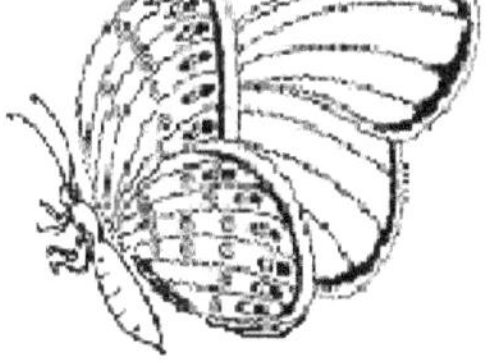

Flower: Purple Lilac
Insect: Karner Blue Butterfly
Mammal: White-tailed Deer, Chinook
Main Rivers: Merrimack, Connecticut

Bird: Purple Finch
Tree: Paper Birch
Soil: Marlow

Fun Facts:

1. The first free public library in the United States was established in 1833 in Peterborough, New Hampshire.
2. The state's license plates—bearing the slogan "Live Free or Die"—are made by prison inmates.
3. The first ever known alien abduction in 1961 happened in Portsmouth when Betty and Barney Hill, announced that they were kidnapped by extraterrestrials and taken into a UFO.
4. The three miles long Cog Railway at Mount Washington is the world's first mountain-climbing cog railway.
5. In 1719, a group of Scotch-Irish immigrants settled in Nutfield (later called Londonderry). These settlers planted what would later become the first potato crop in North America!

Cannon Mountain Aerial Tramway & Franconia Notch

New Jersey

State Name:	New Jersey
Capital:	Trenton
Abbreviations:	NJ; N.J.
Nickname:	The Garden State
Other Names:	Clam State;
	Camden State;
	Amboy State;
	Crossroads of the Revolution
Motto:	Liberty and prosperity
Statehood:	December 18, 1787 (3rd)
Demonym:	New Jerseyan
Time Zone:	Eastern Standard Time
Region/Div:	Northeast / Middle Atlantic
Slogan:	Garden State
Song:	"I'm From New Jersey"
Name Origin:	From the Channel Isle of Jersey in the English Channel
Brief History:	New Jersey was one of the original thirteen colonies that joined the American Revolution for independence from Great Britain. On December 18, 1787, New Jersey ratified the United States Constitution, and on November 20, 1789, New Jersey became the first state in the Nation to ratify the United States Bill of Rights.

Flag

Seal

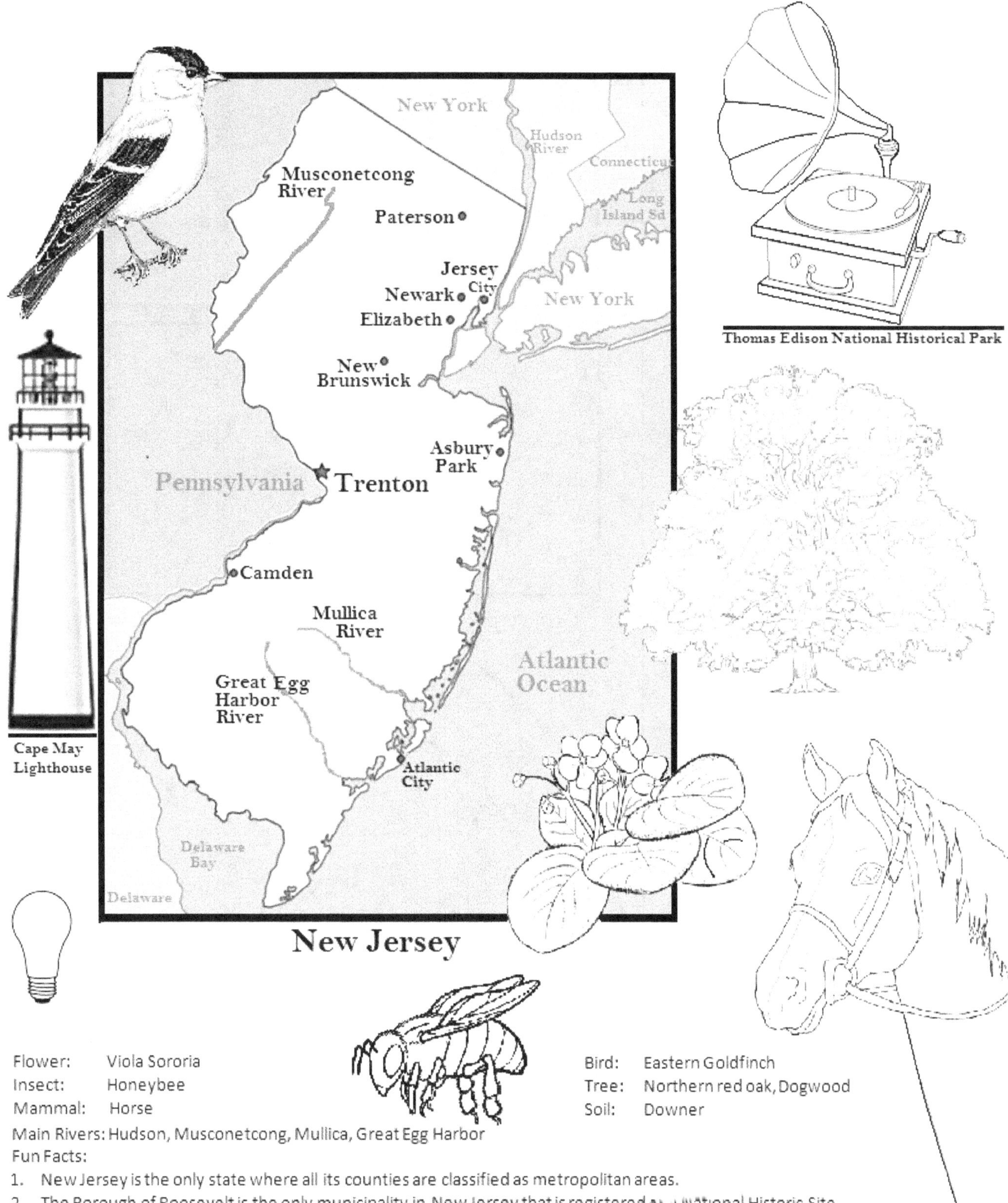

Flower:	Viola Sororia	Bird:	Eastern Goldfinch
Insect:	Honeybee	Tree:	Northern red oak, Dogwood
Mammal:	Horse	Soil:	Downer

Main Rivers: Hudson, Musconetcong, Mullica, Great Egg Harbor

Fun Facts:

1. New Jersey is the only state where all its counties are classified as metropolitan areas.
2. The Borough of Roosevelt is the only municipality in New Jersey that is registered as a National Historic Site.
3. The first Indian reservation was established in New Jersey on August 29, 1758. It was called Brotherton Indian Reservation founded for the Lenni Lenape tribe.
4. Ellis Island was long considered part of New York, but a 1998 United States Supreme Court decision found that most of the island is in New Jersey, 24 of the 27 acres that make up Ellis Island are in New Jersey.
5. The phonograph, light bulb, and motion picture projector were all invented in Thomas Edison's laboratory in Menlo Park, New Jersey.

New Mexico

State Name:	New Mexico
Capital:	Santa Fe
Abbreviations:	NM; N.M.
Nickname:	The Land of Enchantment
Other Names:	New Andalusia; Cactus State; The Outer Space State; The Spanish State
Motto:	It grows as it goes
Statehood:	January 6, 1912 (47th)
Demonym:	New Mexican
Time Zone:	Mountain Standard Time
Region/Div:	West / Mountain
Slogan:	Everybody is somebody in New Mexico
Song:	"O Fair New Mexico"
Name Origin:	Named Nuevo Mexico by the Spanish as early as 1561. The name was anglicized when it was ceded to the United States by Mexico after the Mexican American war.
Brief History:	New Mexico was once part of Mexico until half of it was ceded to the United States after the Mexican-American War with The Treaty of Guadalupe Hidalgo on February 2, 1848. The 1850 Compromise organized the Territory of New Mexico but was denied statehood. In 1863, New Mexico was partitioned into two, the other half became the Territory of Arizona.

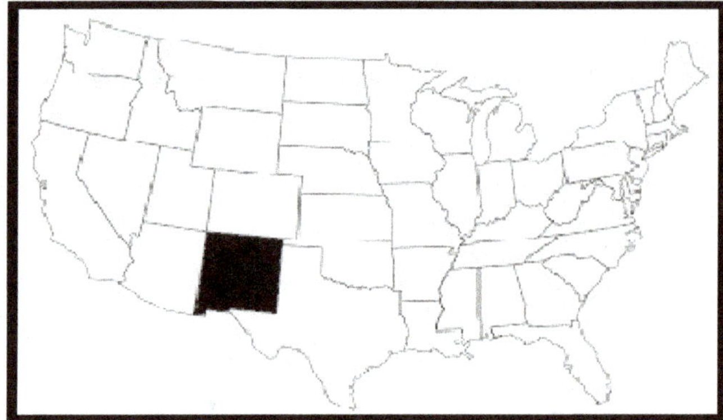

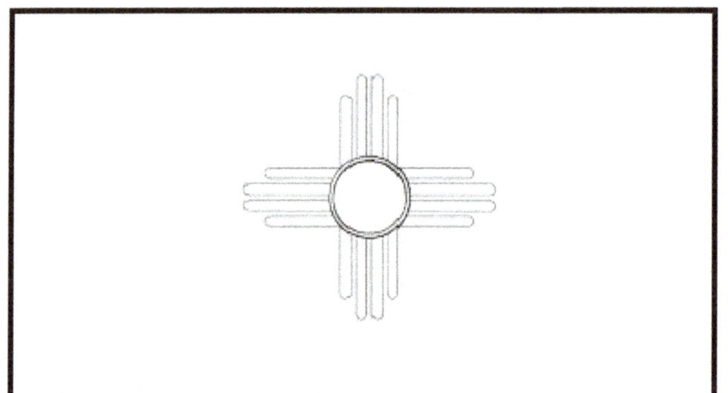

Flag

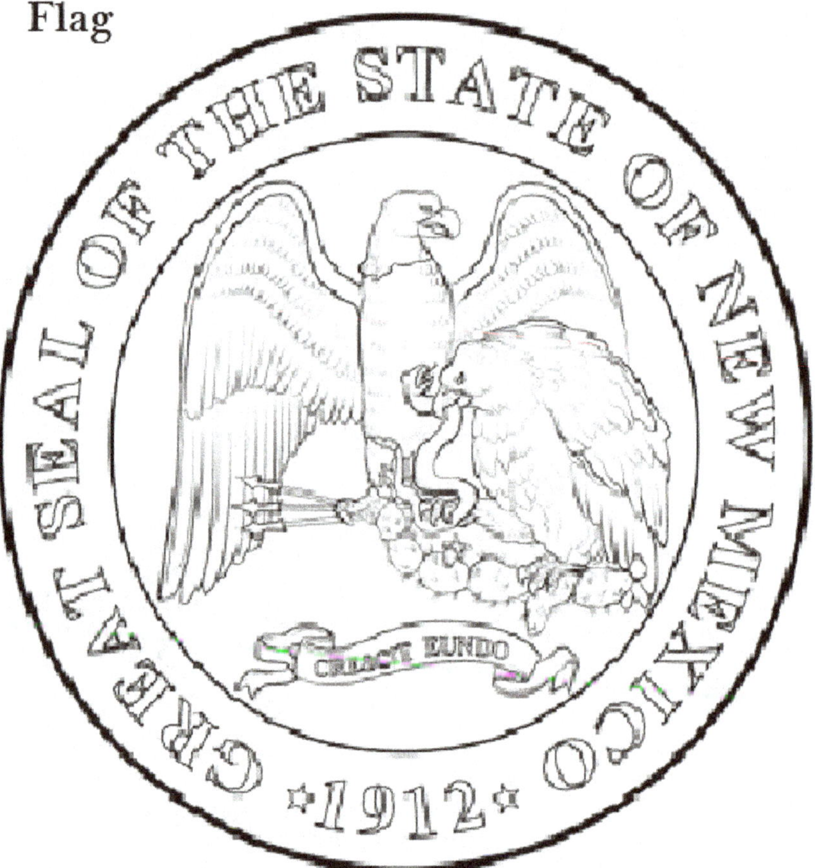

Seal

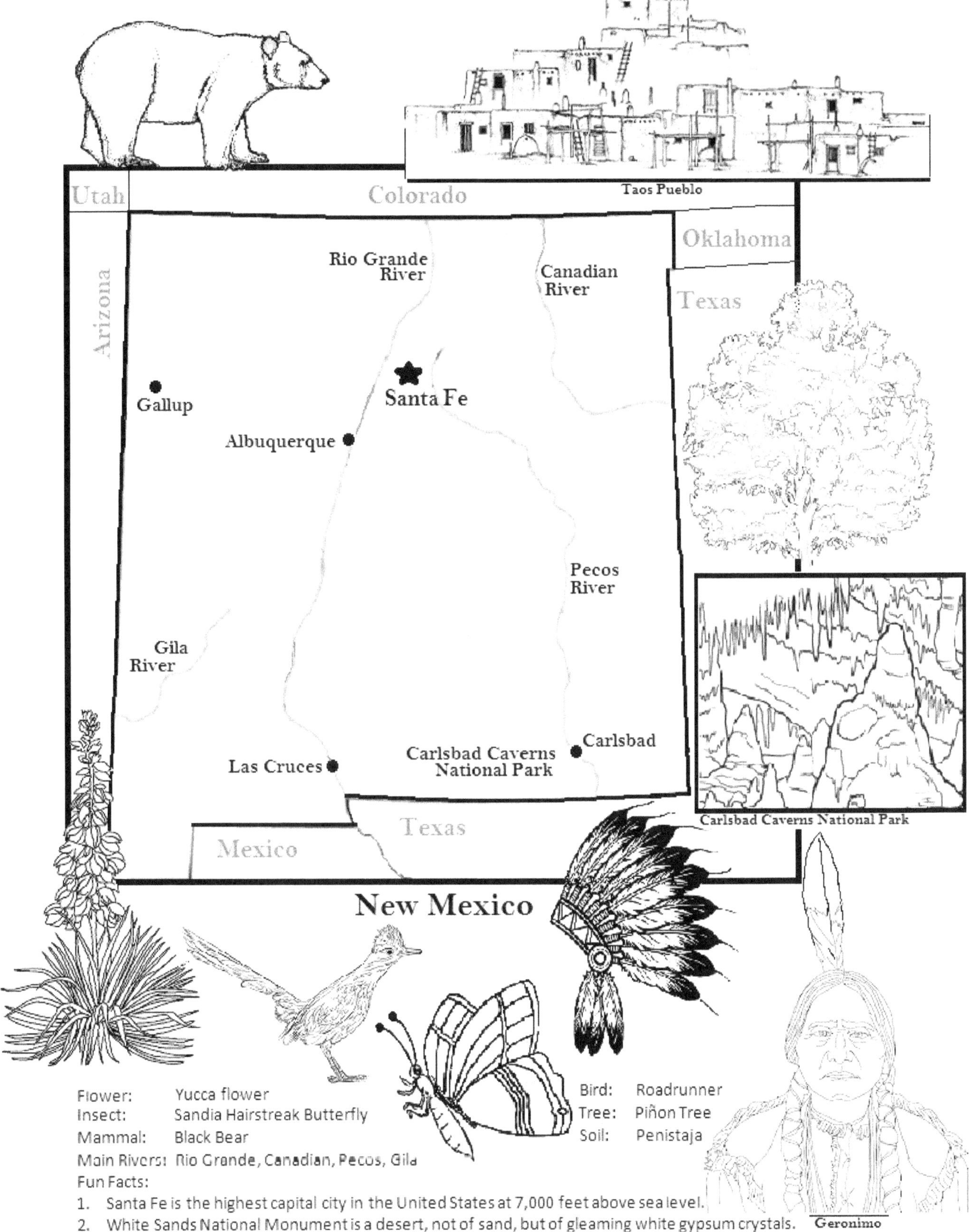

Flower: Yucca flower
Insect: Sandia Hairstreak Butterfly
Mammal: Black Bear
Main Rivers: Rio Grande, Canadian, Pecos, Gila

Bird: Roadrunner
Tree: Piñon Tree
Soil: Penistaja

Fun Facts:

1. Santa Fe is the highest capital city in the United States at 7,000 feet above sea level.
2. White Sands National Monument is a desert, not of sand, but of gleaming white gypsum crystals.
3. The City of Truth or Consequences was once called Hot Springs. In 1950 the town changed its name to the title of a popular radio quiz program.
4. The town of Gallup known as the "Indian Capital of the World", is a trading center for more than 20 Indian tribes.
5. On July 16, 1945, the first atomic bomb was detonated in the desert sands of the Jornada del Muerto.

New York

State Name:	New York
Capital:	Albany
Abbreviations:	NY; N.Y.
Nickname:	The Empire State
Other Names:	Excelsior State; Knickerbocker State; Gateway to the West
Motto:	Ever upwards
Statehood:	July 26, 1788 (11th)
Demonym:	New Yorker
Time Zone:	Eastern Standard Time
Region/Div:	Northeast / Middle Atlantic
Slogan:	I Love NY; I Love New York
Song:	"I Love New York"
Name Origin:	The English took over the colony in 1664 during the second Anglo-Dutch War. They changed the name in honor of the Duke of York who later became King James II of England.
Brief History:	During the 1700s, the Dutch occupied the area until the English came in 1664 and took control of the area from the Dutch and renamed it New York. The Sons of Liberty were organized in New York City during the 1760s, largely in response to the oppressive Stamp Act passed by the British Parliament in 1765. New York was the only colony not to vote for independence, as the delegates were not authorized to do so. New York then endorsed the Declaration of Independence on July 9, 1776. New York State was one of the original thirteen colonies that joined the American Revolution against Great Britain and formed the United States.

Flag

Seal

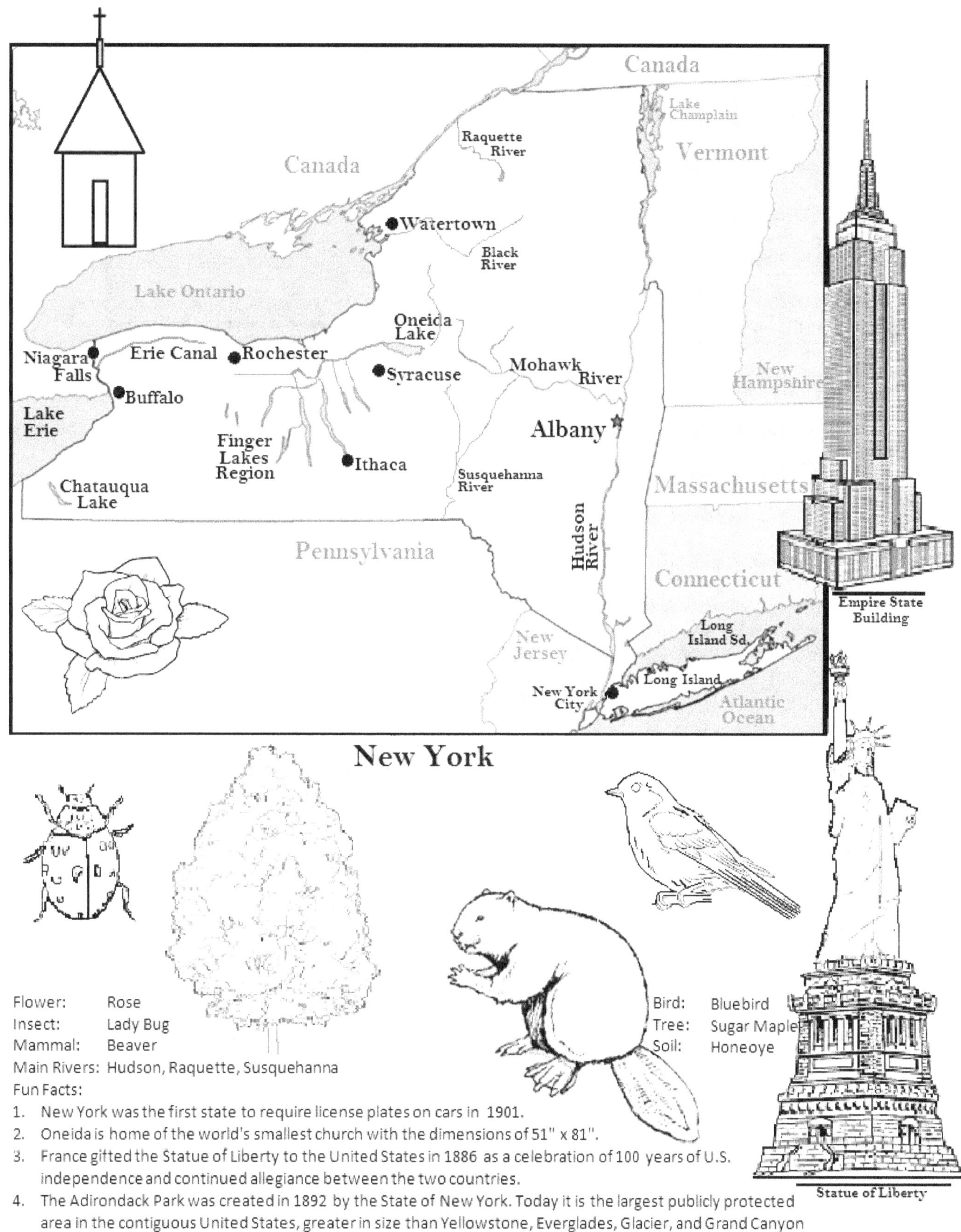

New York

Flower: Rose
Insect: Lady Bug
Mammal: Beaver
Main Rivers: Hudson, Raquette, Susquehanna

Bird: Bluebird
Tree: Sugar Maple
Soil: Honeoye

Fun Facts:

1. New York was the first state to require license plates on cars in 1901.
2. Oneida is home of the world's smallest church with the dimensions of 51" x 81".
3. France gifted the Statue of Liberty to the United States in 1886 as a celebration of 100 years of U.S. independence and continued allegiance between the two countries.
4. The Adirondack Park was created in 1892 by the State of New York. Today it is the largest publicly protected area in the contiguous United States, greater in size than Yellowstone, Everglades, Glacier, and Grand Canyon National Park combined.
5. The first capital of the United States was New York City. In 1789 George Washington took his oath as president on the balcony at Federal Hall.

North Carolina

State Name:	North Carolina
Capital:	Raleigh
Abbreviations:	NC; N.C.
Nickname:	The Tar Heel State
Other Names:	The Old North State;
	First in Flight;
	Land of the Sky;
	Rip Van Winkle State
Motto:	To be rather than to seem
Statehood:	November 21, 1789 (12th)
Demonym:	North Carolinian
Time Zone:	Eastern Standard Time
Region/Div:	South / South Atlantic
Slogan:	Drive Safely;
	First in Freedom;
	First in Flight
Song:	"The Old North State"
Name Origin:	Named after King Charles I and King Charles II of England. The name "Carolina" comes from the Latin word "Carolinus," meaning "of Charles."
Brief History:	The Spanish established Fort San Juan in 1567 at the site of the Native American community of Joara but the fort lasted only 18 months. The natives decimated the Spaniards. In 1729, North Carolina became one of the English Thirteen Colonies and with the territory of South Carolina was originally known as the Province of Carolina. On November 21, 1789, North Carolina becomes the 12th state of the United States of America. On May 20, 1861, North Carolina left the Union, North Carolina voted to "undo" the act that had brought it into the United States. However on July 4, 1868 North Carolina was readmitted to the Union.

Flag

Seal

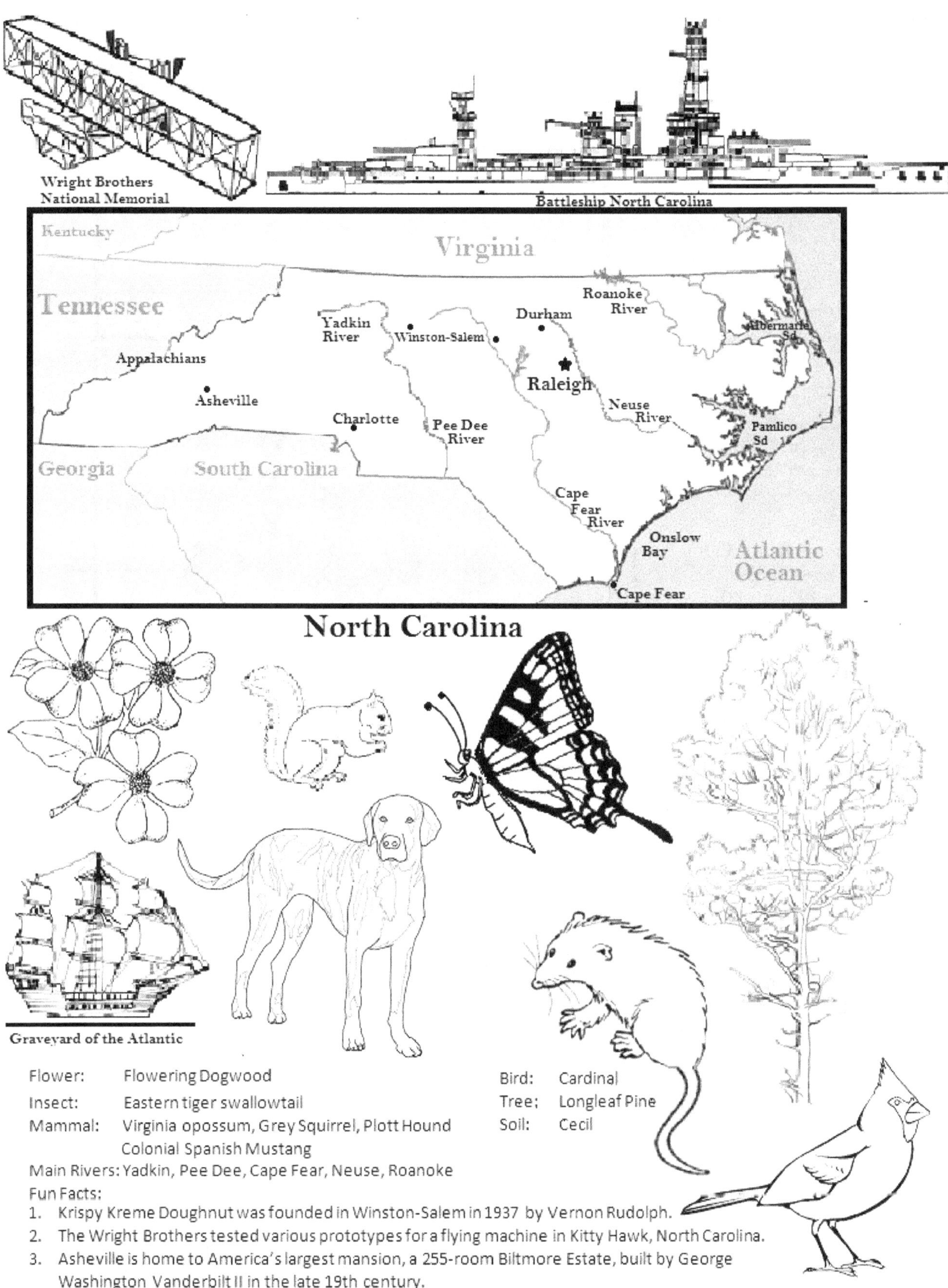

North Carolina

Flower: Flowering Dogwood

Insect: Eastern tiger swallowtail

Mammal: Virginia opossum, Grey Squirrel, Plott Hound Colonial Spanish Mustang

Bird: Cardinal

Tree;   Longleaf Pine

Soil: Cecil

Main Rivers: Yadkin, Pee Dee, Cape Fear, Neuse, Roanoke

Fun Facts:

1. Krispy Kreme Doughnut was founded in Winston-Salem in 1937 by Vernon Rudolph.

2. The Wright Brothers tested various prototypes for a flying machine in Kitty Hawk, North Carolina.

3. Asheville is home to America's largest mansion, a 255-room Biltmore Estate, built by George Washington Vanderbilt II in the late 19th century.

4. In 1893, Pepsi-Cola was born in New Bern, North Carolina. Originally called "Brad's Drink, was invented by a drugstore clerk named Caleb Bradham.

5. The High Tider (Hoi Toider) dialect is only spoken in North Carolina's Outer Banks and Pamlico Sound regions.

North Dakota

State Name:	North Dakota
Capital:	Bismarck
Abbreviations:	ND; N. Dak.
Nickname:	The Peace Garden State
Other Names:	Roughrider State; Flickertail State; Sioux State; The Great Central State
Motto:	Liberty and union, now and forever, one and inseparable
Statehood:	November 2, 1889 (39th)
Demonym:	North Dakotan
Time Zone:	Central Standard Time; Southwestern part of the State Name: Mountain Standard Time
Region/Div:	Midwest / West North Central
Slogan:	Peace Garden State; Discover the Spirit
Song:	"North Dakota Hymn"
Name Origin:	North and South Dakota were one territory until 1889. Dakota was named after Dakota a Sioux tribe which lived in the region. Dakota is the Sioux word for "friends" or "allies."
Brief History:	From 1762 to 1802 the region was part of Spanish Louisiana. In 1861, the area that is now North Dakota was incorporated into the new Dakota Territory along with what is now South Dakota. The Dakota Territory (1861 - 1889), consisted part of the land acquired in the Louisiana purchase in 1803, and part of Rupert's Land, which was acquired in 1818 when the boundary was changed to the 49th parallel. On November 2, 1889, North Dakota and South Dakota became separate states. Congress passed an omnibus bill for statehood for North Dakota titled the Enabling Act of 1889.

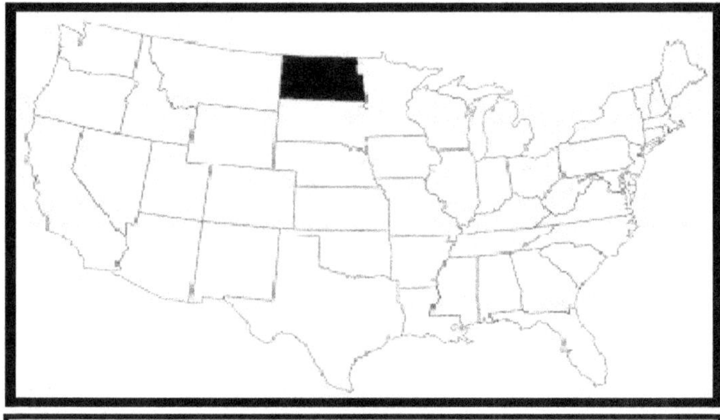

Flag

Seal

North Dakota

Flower: Wild Prairie Rose
Insect: Convergent Lady Beetle (Ladybug)
Mammal: The Nokota Horse
Main Rivers: James, Missouri, Little Missouri

Bird: Western Meadowlark
Tree: American Elm
Soil: Williams

Fun Facts:

1.   North Dakota was the first state to complete its Interstate highway system.
2.   In 1881, David Henderson Houston from Hunter filed a patent on the first roll film camera, invented by his brother Peter. Eight years later he sold the patent to George Eastman, and suggested the name Nodak, an abbreviation of No[rth] Dak[ota], but Eastman decided to change the initial "N" to a "K,".
3.   The town of Rugby is the geographical center of North America. A 15 foot tall rock obelisk flanked by poles flying the United States and Canadian flags marks the location.
4.   New Salem, North Dakota is home to Salem Sue, the "World's Largest Holstein Cow" built to honor the dairymen of the area. Standing 38 feet tall, Sue is 50 feet long and weighs about six tons.
5.   The world's largest buffalo monument is located at Frontier Village in Jamestown. Built in 1959, it is 26 foot tall, 46 foot long, and weighs a whopping 60 tons!

Knife River Indian Villages
National Historic Site

Ohio

State Name:	Ohio
Capital:	Columbus
Abbreviations:	OH; Oh.
Nickname:	The Buckeye State
Other Names:	Mother of Modern Presidents; Birthplace of Aviation
Motto:	With God all things are possible
Statehood:	March 1, 1803 (17th)
Demonym:	Ohioan
Time Zone:	Eastern Standard Time
Region/Div:	Midwest / East North Central
Slogan:	Seat Belts Fastened?; The Heart of It All!; Birthplace of Aviation
Song:	"Beautiful Ohio"
Name Origin:	From the Ohio River. The name originated from the Seneca language word ohi:yo', meaning "great river" or "large creek".
Brief History:	During the 18th century, the French set up a system of trading posts to control the fur trade in the region. Beginning in 1754, France and Great Britain fought the French and Indian War also known as the Seven Years' War. As a result of the Treaty of Paris, the French ceded control of Ohio and the remainder of the Old Northwest to Great Britain. When the Americans won the Revolutionary War in 1783, the British ceded claims to Ohio. In 1787, the United States of America created the Northwest Territory also known as the Territory Northwest of the River Ohio. Then, the Enabling Act of 1802 was passed by Congress to define the process for Ohio to seek statehood.

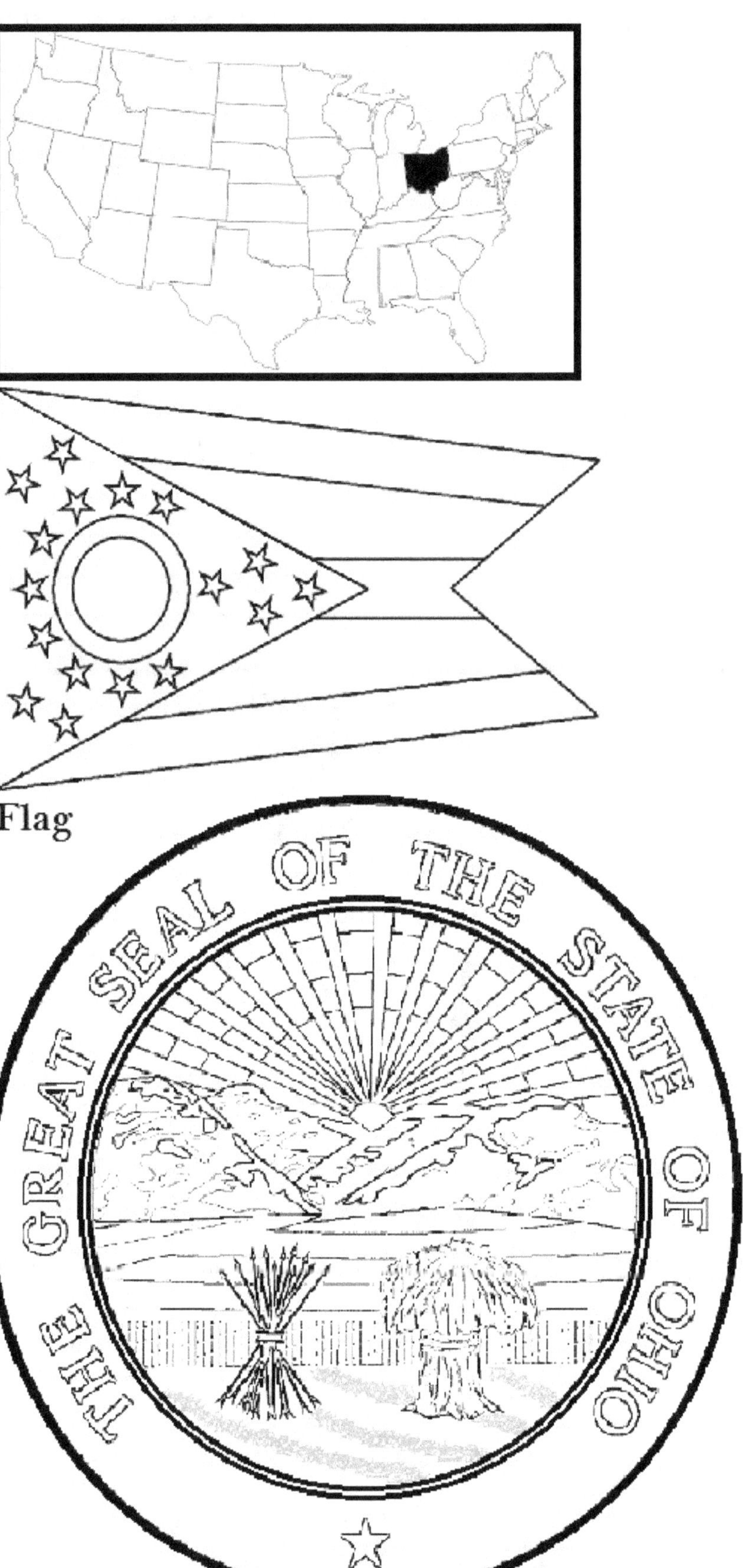

Flag

Seal

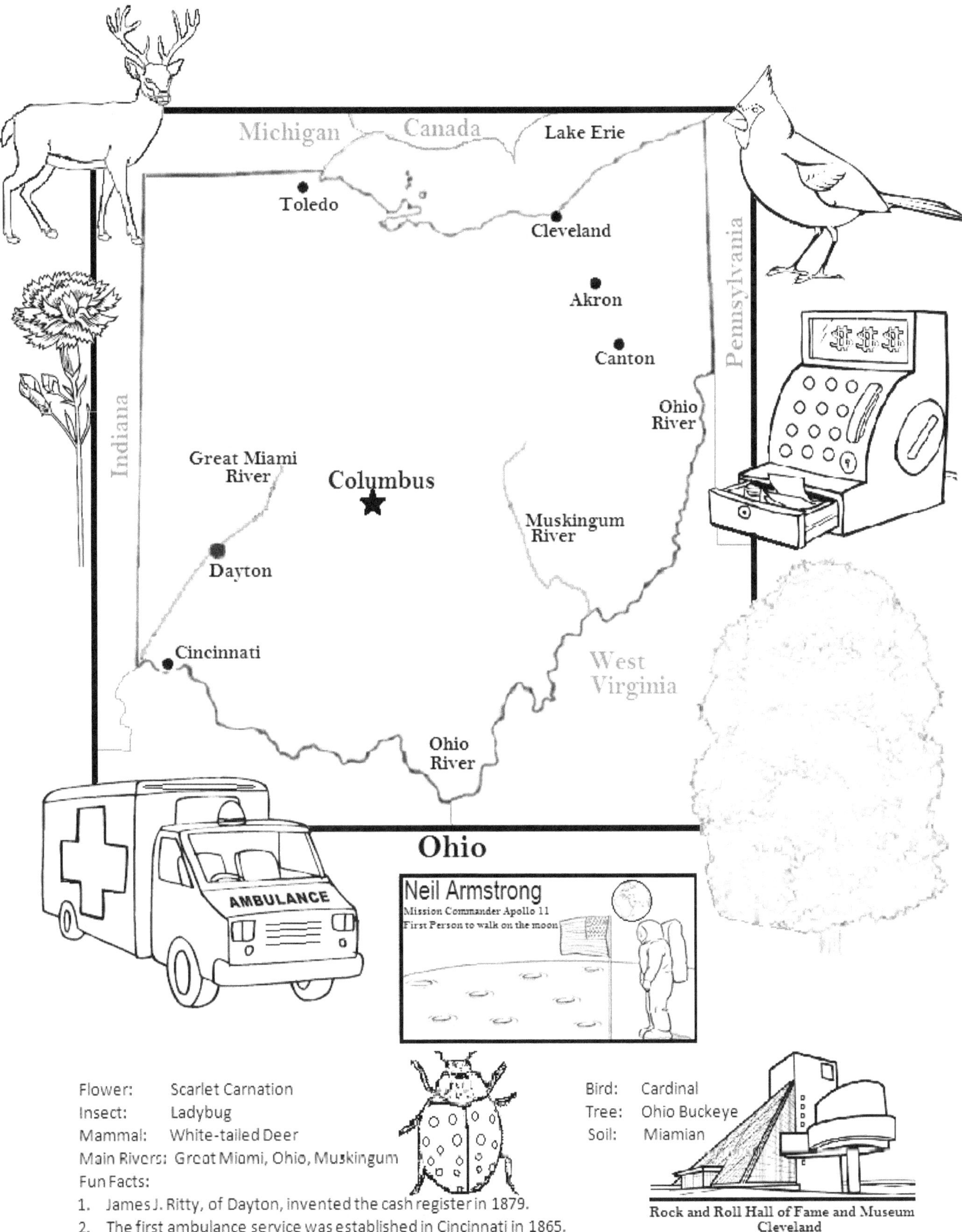

Flower: Scarlet Carnation
Insect: Ladybug
Mammal: White-tailed Deer
Main Rivers: Great Miami, Ohio, Muskingum

Bird: Cardinal
Tree: Ohio Buckeye
Soil: Miamian

Fun Facts:

1. James J. Ritty, of Dayton, invented the cash register in 1879.
2. The first ambulance service was established in Cincinnati in 1865.
3. Neil Armstrong, the first man to walk on the moon, was from Wapakoneta.
4. John Lambert of Ohio City made America's first gasoline automobile in 1891.
5. The Great Serpent Mound, the largest serpent effigy in the world at a half mile long, is on a plateau overlooking Brush Creek Valley in Adams County.

Oklahoma

State Name:	Oklahoma
Capital:	Oklahoma City
Abbreviations:	OK; Okla.
Nickname:	The Sooner State
Other Names:	Boomer's Paradise; Land of the Red Man
Motto:	Labor conquers all things
Statehood:	November 16, 1907 (46th
Demonym:	Oklahoman
Time Zone:	Central Standard Time
Region/Div:	South / West South Central
Slogan:	Visit; Is OK!; Native America
Song:	"Oklahoma"

Name Origin: From the Choctaw words "okla" and "humma," meaning "red people." A Choctaw Chief suggested the Oklahoma name during treaty negotiations referring to the people's skin color.

Brief History: French explorers claimed the area in the 1700s. In the 18th century, Kiowa, Apache, and Comanche entered the region from the west and Quapaw and Osage peoples moved into what is now eastern Oklahoma. French colonists claimed the region until 1803, when all the French territory west of the Mississippi River was sold to the United States. The areas of Oklahoma east of its panhandle were acquired in the Louisiana Purchase of 1803. In 1845, the Western Panhandle region became US territory with the annexation of Texas. In the 1880s, settlers of the Panhandle region tried unsuccessfully to form the Cimarron Territory. The panhandle area was referred to as No Man's Land until statehood decades later.

Flag

Seal

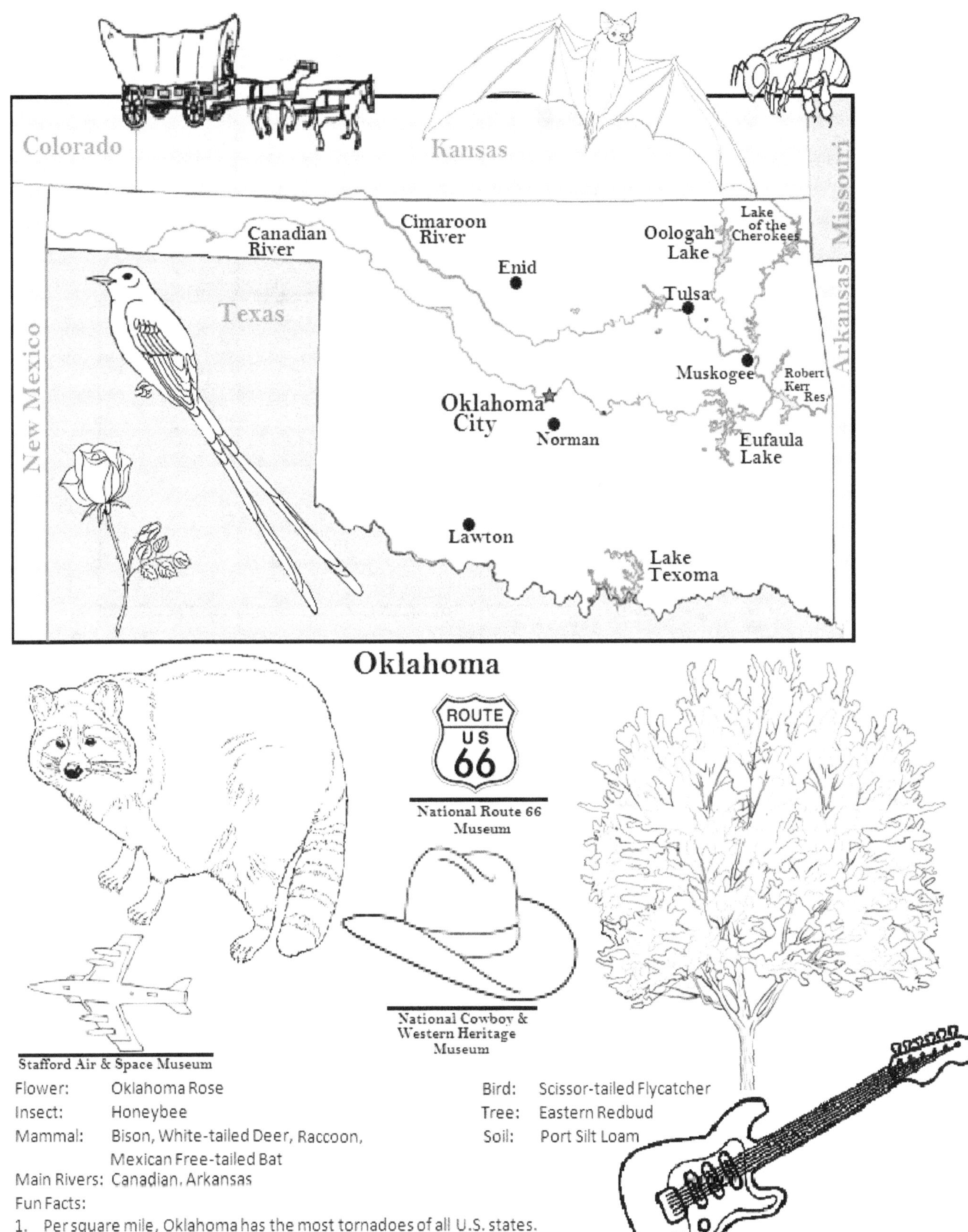

Oklahoma

Flower:	Oklahoma Rose	Bird:	Scissor-tailed Flycatcher
Insect:	Honeybee	Tree:	Eastern Redbud
Mammal:	Bison, White-tailed Deer, Raccoon,	Soil:	Port Silt Loam
	Mexican Free-tailed Bat		

Main Rivers: Canadian, Arkansas

Fun Facts:

1. Per square mile, Oklahoma has the most tornadoes of all U.S. states.
2. Bob Dunn a musician from Beggs invented the first electric guitar 1935.
3. The world's first parking meter was installed in Oklahoma City on July 16, 1935.
4. Oklahoma has the largest Native American population in the U.S. It is tribal headquarters for 39 tribes.
5. The Oklahoma State Capitol is the only capitol in the world surrounded by working oil wells. Not too many years ago, giant oil rigs dotted the grounds of the Oklahoma capitol.

Oregon

State Name:	Oregon
Capital:	Salem
Abbreviations:	OR; Ore.
Nickname:	The Beaver State
Other Names:	Webfoot State; Union State; The Sunset State
Motto:	She flies with her own wings
Statehood:	February 14, 1859 (33rd)
Demonym:	Oregonian
Time Zone:	Central Time Zone
Region/Div:	Pacific Standard Time; Part of Malheur County: Mountain Standard Time
Slogan:	Pacific Wonderland
Song:	"Oregon, My Oregon"
Name Origin:	One theory has it that the name comes from the French Canadian word "ouragan" meaning "storm" or "hurricane." It's thought that the Columbia River was at one time called "the river of storms".
Brief History:	Great Britain and the U.S. both claimed ownership of Oregon. The joint occupation of the British and the U.S. ended with the signing of the Oregon Treaty in 1846, when Britain and the U.S. split the disputed region equally, along present borders, with the U.S. generally receiving lands south of the 49th parallel. The Oregon Territory was established on August 14, 1848. Federally-appointed Governor Joseph Lane proclaimed that Oregon is now a Territory of the United States.

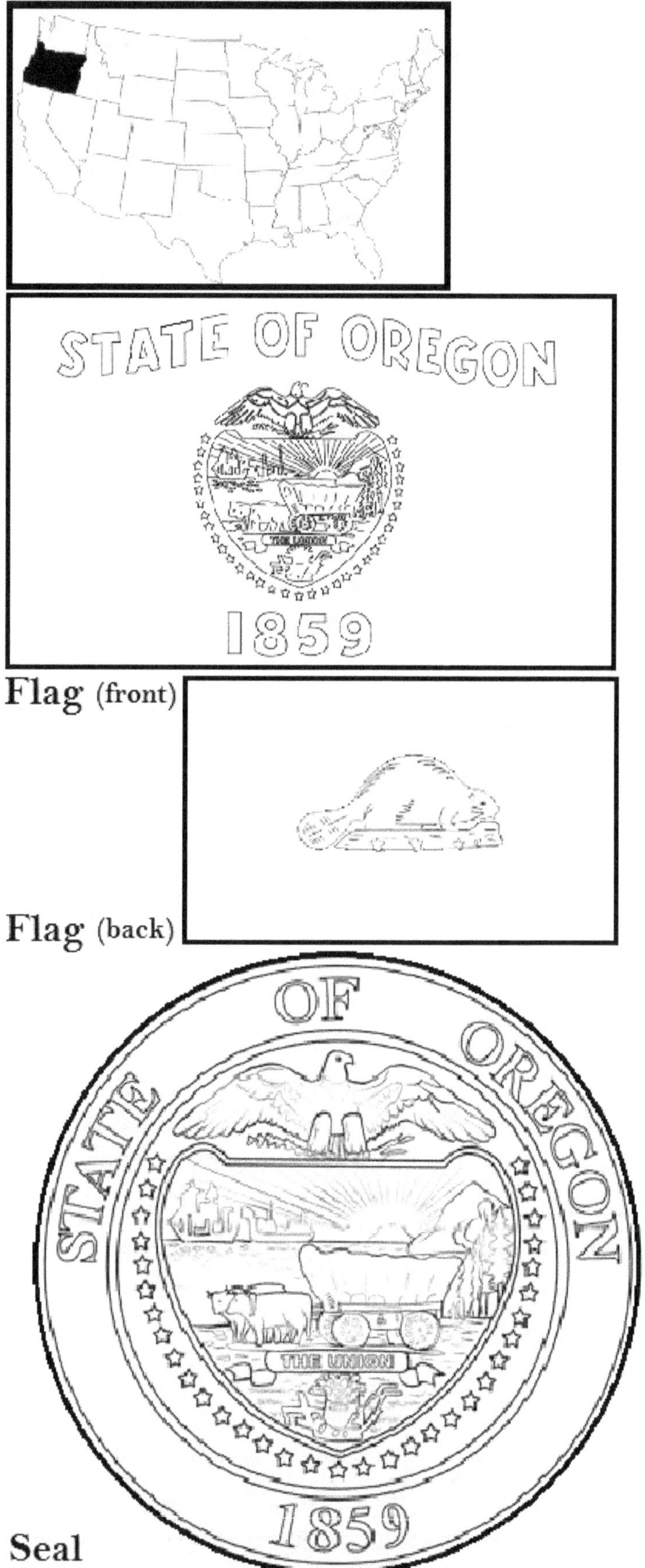

Flag (front)

Flag (back)

Seal

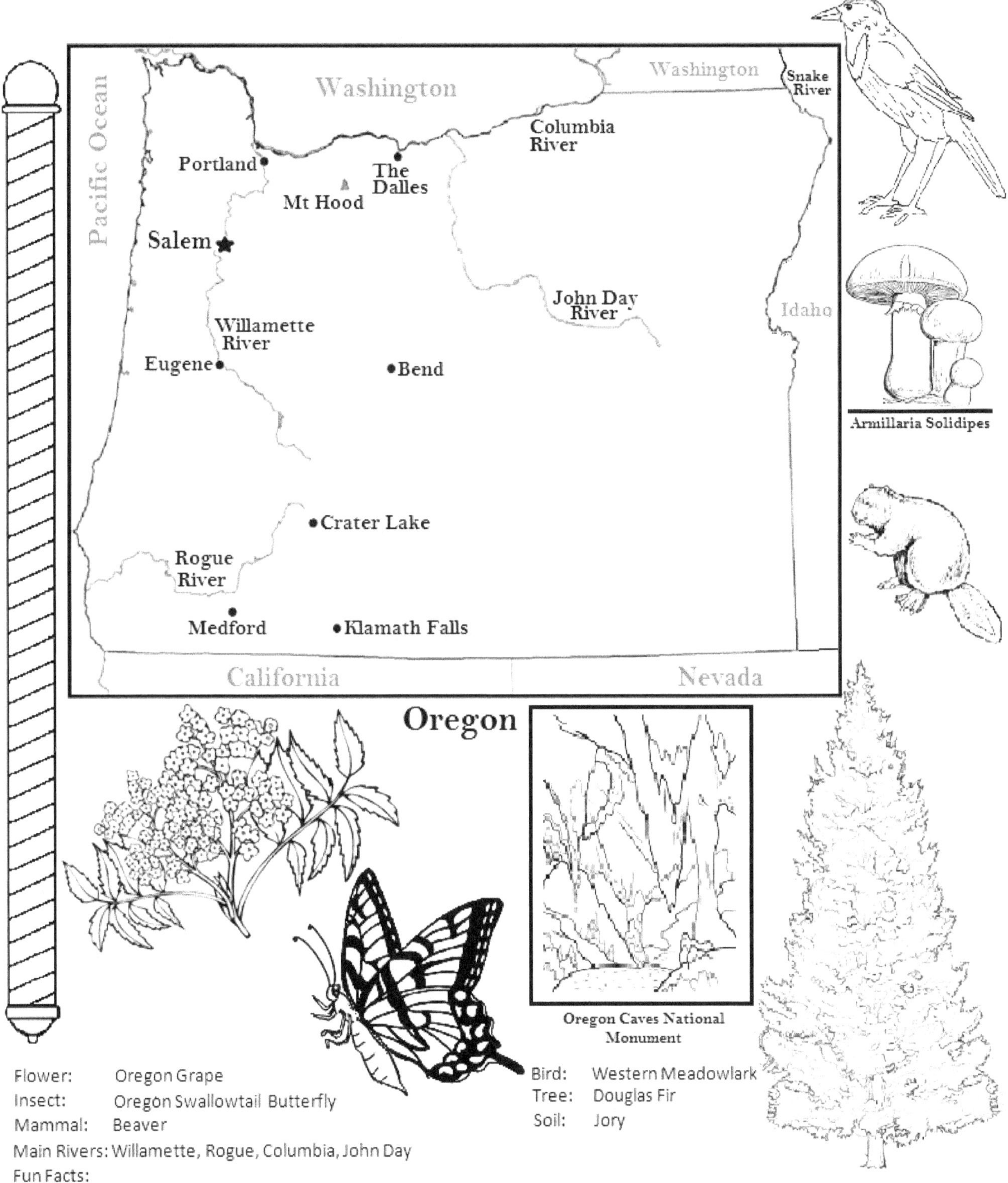

Flower:	Oregon Grape	
Insect:	Oregon Swallowtail Butterfly	
Mammal:	Beaver	

Bird:	Western Meadowlark
Tree:	Douglas Fir
Soil:	Jory

Main Rivers: Willamette, Rogue, Columbia, John Day

Fun Facts:

1. Oregon is home to the world's shortest river. The D River is only 121 feet long.
2. The Malheur National Forest contains the largest known organism (by area) in the world: an Armillaria solidipes that spans 2,200 acres and has been growing for about 2,400 years.
3. Oregon's state flag pictures a beaver on its reverse side. It is the only state flag to carry two separate designs.
4. Forest Grove is home to the world's tallest barber pole. Built in 1973, the red, white, and blue striped pole is 72 feet high
5. During the Great Depression, North Bend used wooden coins as currency. The coins are still considered legal tender, though they're coveted by coin collectors and rarely spent.

Pennsylvania

State Name:	Commonwealth of Pennsylvania
Capital:	Harrisburg
Abbreviations:	PA; Pa.
Nickname:	The Keystone State
Other Names:	Quaker State; The Commonwealth; Independence State
Motto:	Virtue, liberty, and independence
Statehood:	December 12, 1787 (2nd)
Demonym:	Pennsylvanian
Time Zone:	Eastern Standard Time
Region/Div:	Northeast / Middle Atlantic
Slogan:	Keystone State; You've Got a Friend In
Song:	"Pennsylvania"
Name Origin:	After Admiral Sir William Penn, father of William Penn. It means "Penn's Woodland"
Brief History:	Pennsylvania was colonized by Swedish and Dutch settlers before the English took control of the colony in 1667. On March 4, 1681, Charles II of England granted the Province of Pennsylvania to William Penn to settle a debt the king owed to Penn's father. The western portions of Pennsylvania were disputed by the British and French during the French and Indian War. Pennsylvania was one of the thirteen colonies that rebelled against the British rule during the American Revolution. It was the site of the first and second Continental Congress in 1774 and 1775. It was at Independence Hall in Philadelphia where the Declaration of Independence was signed in 1776. In 1787, Pennsylvania ratifies the Constitution and becomes the 2nd state.

Flag

Seal

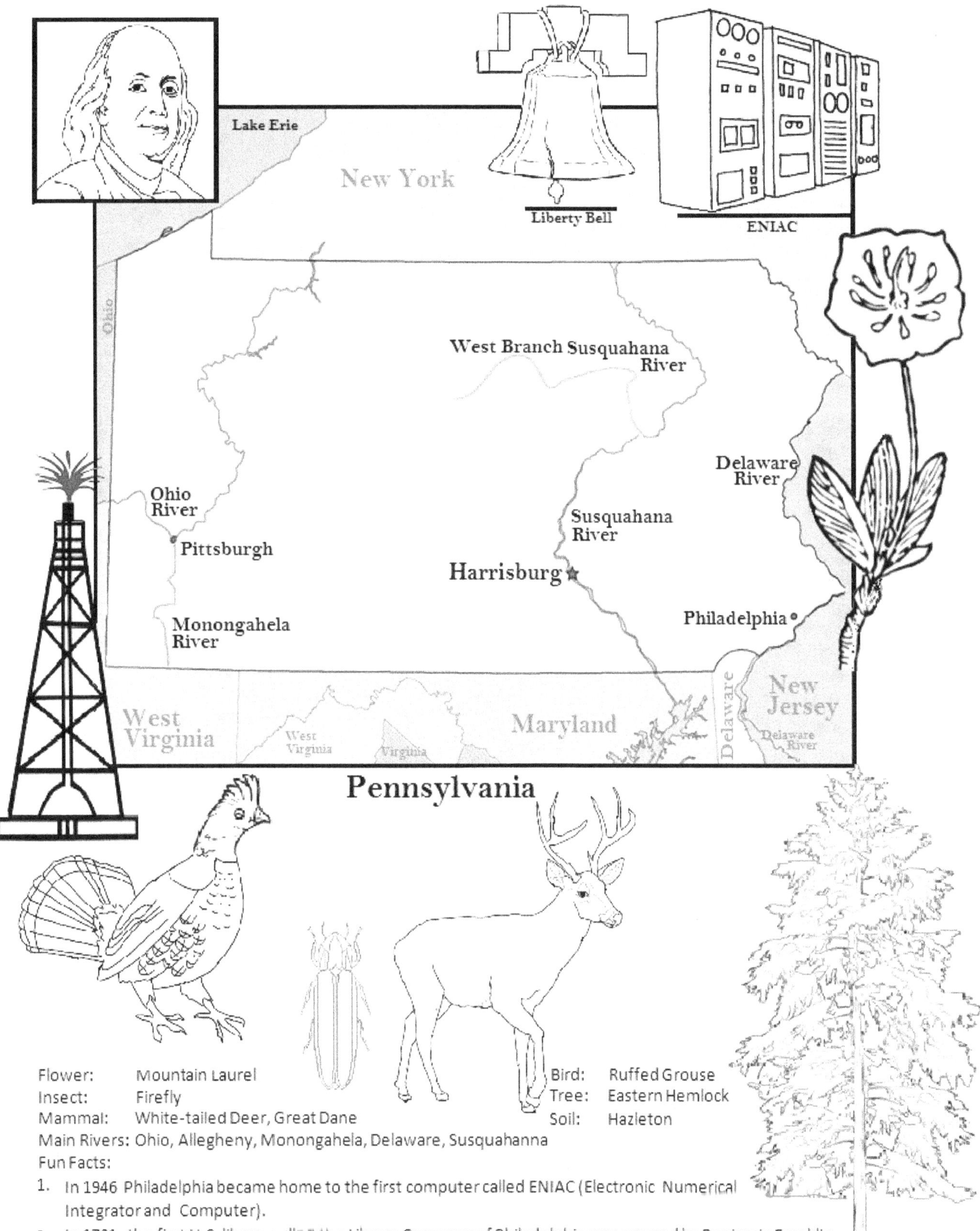

Flower: Mountain Laurel
Insect: Firefly
Mammal: White-tailed Deer, Great Dane
Bird: Ruffed Grouse
Tree: Eastern Hemlock
Soil: Hazleton
Main Rivers: Ohio, Allegheny, Monongahela, Delaware, Susquahanna
Fun Facts:

1. In 1946 Philadelphia became home to the first computer called ENIAC (Electronic Numerical Integrator and Computer).
2. In 1731, the first U.S. library called the Library Company of Philadelphia was opened by Benjamin Franklin.
3. In 1953, Dr. Jonas Salk discovers the vaccine for polio while working at the University of Pittsburgh.
4. Philadelphia is home to the Liberty Bell. This state's name is spelled Pensylvania on the Liberty Bell. The Constitution uses one n in one section and two n's in another.
5. In 1859, near Titusville, Pennsylvania, Edwin Drake successfully drilled the well, the first commercially drilled oil well, which led to the first major oil boom in United States history.

Rhode Island

State Name:	Rhode Island and Providence Plantations
Capital:	Providence
Abbreviations:	RI; R.I.
Nickname:	The Ocean State
Other Names:	Plantation State; The Smallest State; Little Rhody; The Southern Gateway of New England
Motto:	Hope
Statehood:	May 29, 1790 (13th)
Demonym:	Rhode Islander
Time Zone:	Eastern Standard Time
Region/Div:	Northeast / New England
Slogan:	Discover; Ocean State
Song:	"Rhode Island, It's for Me"
Name Origin:	Giovanni da Verrazzano, the explorer, dated July 8, 1524, in which he refers to an island near the mouth of Narragansett Bay, and likens the island to the Island Rhodes in the Aegean Sea.
	This state was named by Dutch explorer Adrian Block. He named it "Roodt Eylandt" meaning "red island" in reference to the red clay that lined the shore. The name was later anglicized when the region came under British rule.
Brief History:	Rhode Island was founded by Roger Williams in 1636, who had been banished from the Massachusetts colony. On May 4, 1776 Rhode Island was the first of the thirteen colonies to renounce its allegiance to the British Crown but the last of the thirteen colonies to ratify the United States Constitution.

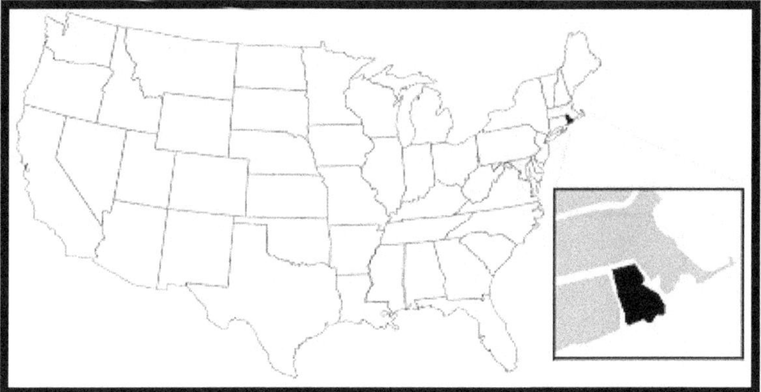

Flag

Seal

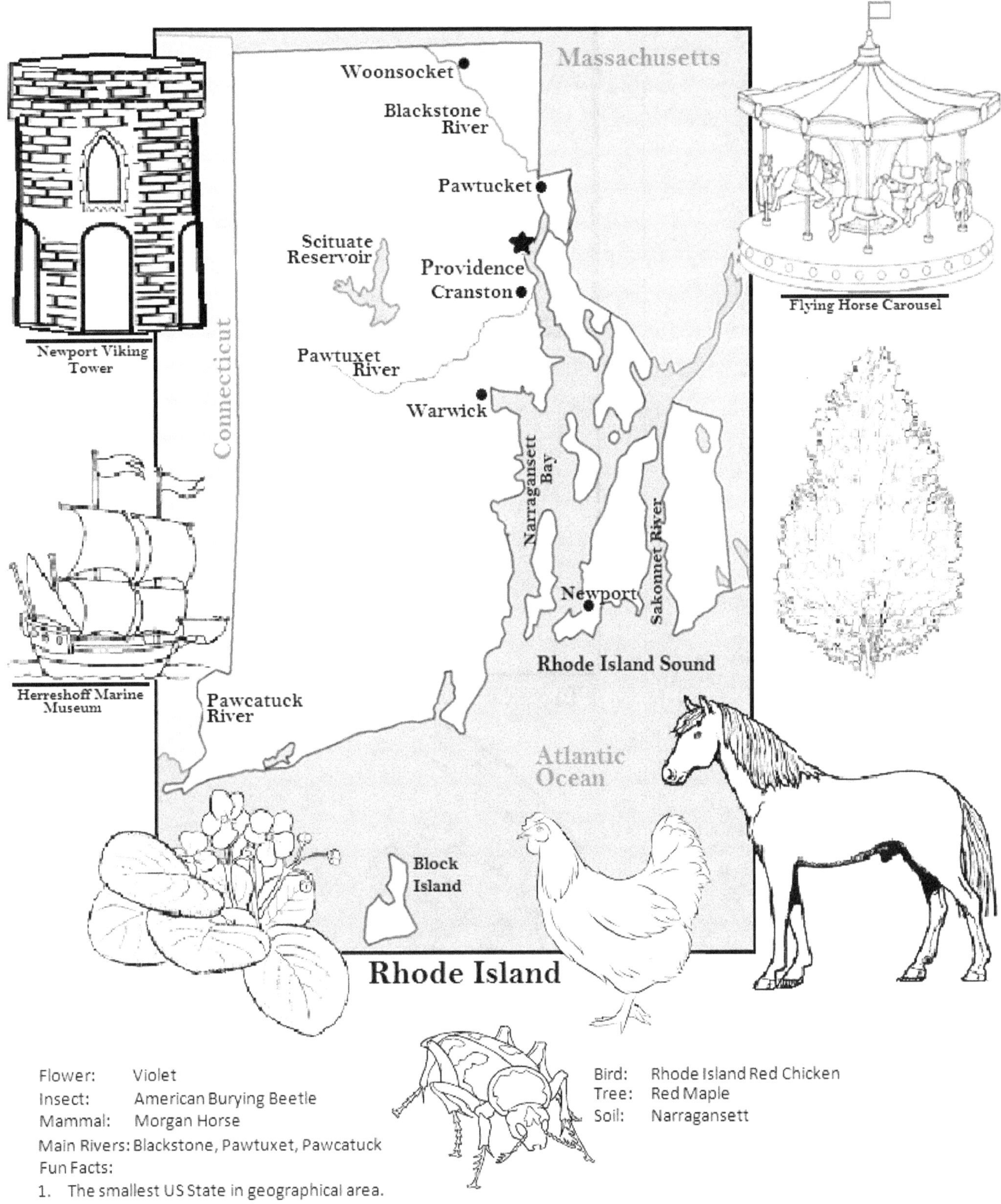

Flower: Violet
Insect: American Burying Beetle
Mammal: Morgan Horse
Main Rivers: Blackstone, Pawtuxet, Pawcatuck

Bird: Rhode Island Red Chicken
Tree: Red Maple
Soil: Narragansett

Fun Facts:

1. The smallest US State in geographical area.

2. The first circus in the United States was in Newport in 1774.

3. The Flying Horse Carousel built in 1850, is the nation's oldest carousel, located in the resort town of Watch Hill.

4. The only state that still celebrates the end of World War II on Victory Day (VJ Day), observed each year on the second Monday of August.

5. Newport may be home to the oldest standing building in America, the Viking Tower in Truro Park, was built sometime during the mid-17th century.

South Carolina

State Name:	South Carolina
Capital:	Columbia
Abbreviations:	SC; S.C.
Nickname:	The Palmetto State
Other Names:	Rice State;
	Iodine State;
	Keystone of the South
	Atlantic Seaboard;
	Swamp State
Motto:	While I breathe, I hope;
	Prepared in Mind and
	Resources
Statehood:	May 23, 1788 (8th)
Demonym:	South Carolinian
Time Zone:	Eastern Standard Time
Region/Div:	South / South Atlantic
Slogan:	The Iodine State;
	The Iodine Products State;
	Smiling Faces;
	Beautiful Places
Song:	"Carolina"
Name Origin:	Carolina is from the Latin word for Charles (Carolus) honoring King Charles I of England (who made the original land grant in 1629). South Carolina was formed in 1729, when the Carolina colony was divided in two.
Brief History:	South Carolina was one of the original thirteen states of the United States. In 1788, South Carolina joins the United States as the eighth state. However, in 1860 South Carolina is the first state to secede from the Union and join the Confederacy. But in 1868, South Carolina was readmitted to the Union.

Flag

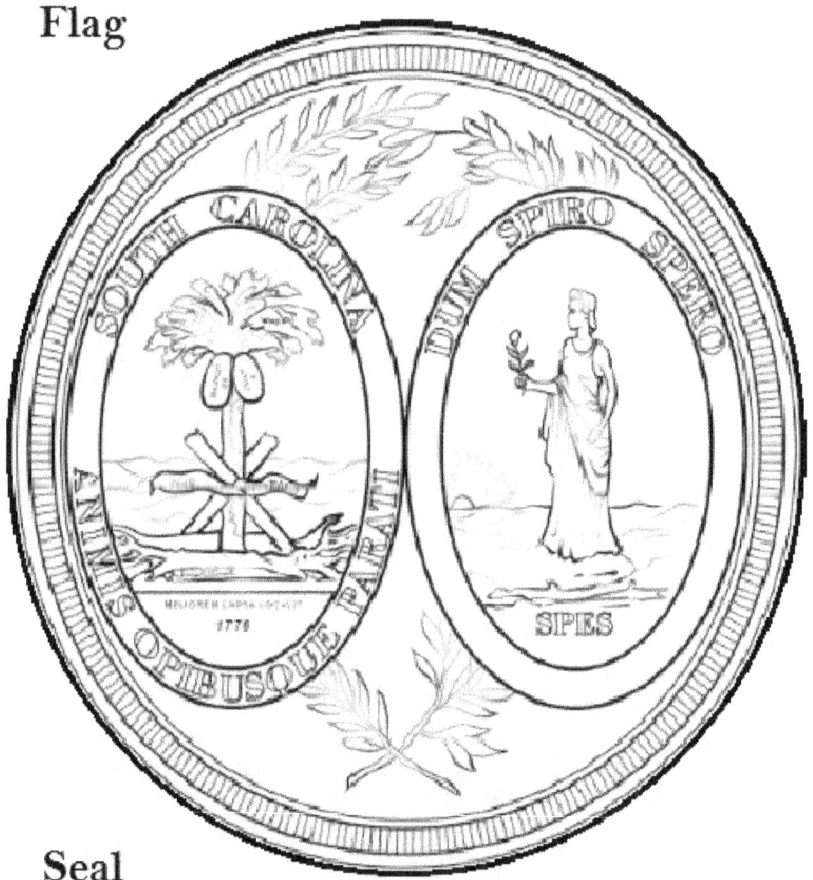

Seal

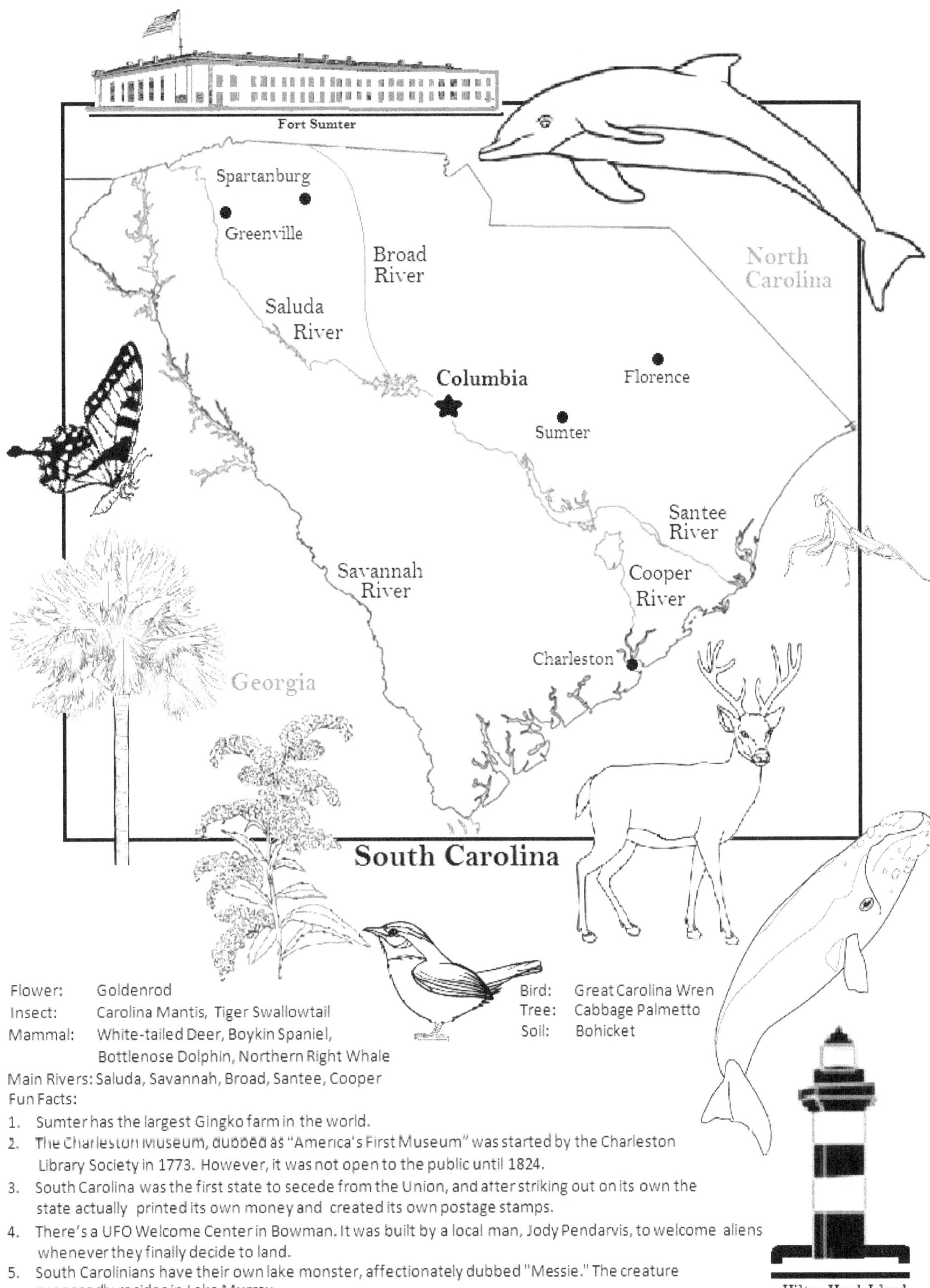

Flower: Goldenrod
Insect: Carolina Mantis, Tiger Swallowtail
Mammal: White-tailed Deer, Boykin Spaniel,
              Bottlenose Dolphin, Northern Right Whale

Bird: Great Carolina Wren
Tree: Cabbage Palmetto
Soil: Bohicket

Main Rivers: Saluda, Savannah, Broad, Santee, Cooper

Fun Facts:

1. Sumter has the largest Gingko farm in the world.
2. The Charleston Museum, dubbed as "America's First Museum" was started by the Charleston Library Society in 1773. However, it was not open to the public until 1824.
3. South Carolina was the first state to secede from the Union, and after striking out on its own the state actually printed its own money and created its own postage stamps.
4. There's a UFO Welcome Center in Bowman. It was built by a local man, Jody Pendarvis, to welcome aliens whenever they finally decide to land.
5. South Carolinians have their own lake monster, affectionately dubbed "Messie." The creature supposedly resides in Lake Murray.

South Dakota

State Name:	South Dakota
Capital:	Pierre
Abbreviations:	SD; S. Dak.
Nickname:	The Mount Rushmore State
Other Names:	Sunshine state; Coyote state; Land of Plenty
Motto:	Under God the people rule
Statehood:	November 2, 1889 (40th)
Demonym:	South Dakotan
Time Zone:	Mountain Standard Time ; Central Standard Time
Region/Div:	Midwest / West North Central
Slogan:	Great Faces; Great Places
Song:	"Hail! South Dakota"
Name Origin:	North and South Dakota were one territory until 1889. Dakota was named after Dakota a Sioux tribe which lived in the region. Dakota is the Sioux word for "friends" or "allies.
Brief History:	The Dakota Territory consisted part of the land acquired in the Louisiana purchase in 1803, and part of Rupert's Land, which was acquired in 1818 when the boundary was changed to the 49th parallel. In 1861, the area that is now North Dakota was incorporated into the new Dakota Territory along with what is now South Dakota. On November 2, 1889, North Dakota and South Dakota became separate states.

Flag

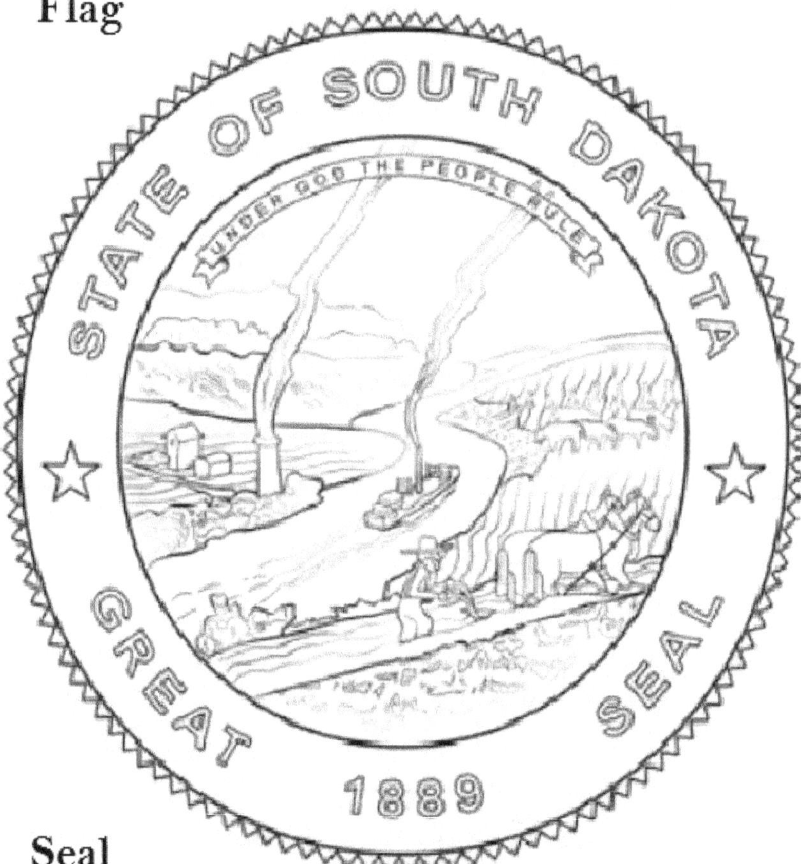

Seal

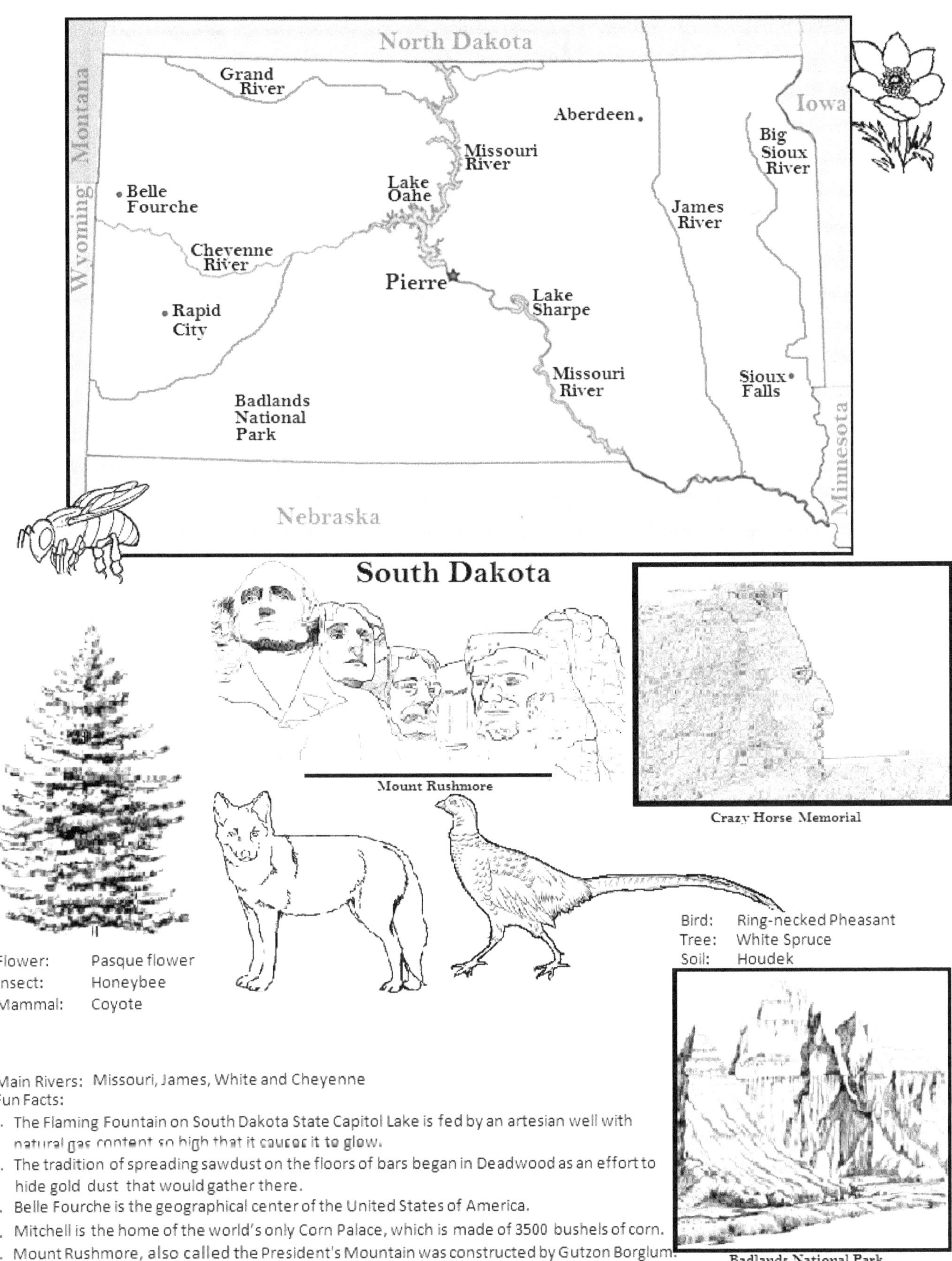

South Dakota

Mount Rushmore

Crazy Horse Memorial

Flower: Pasque flower
Insect: Honeybee
Mammal: Coyote

Bird: Ring-necked Pheasant
Tree: White Spruce
Soil: Houdek

Badlands National Park

Main Rivers: Missouri, James, White and Cheyenne

Fun Facts:

1. The Flaming Fountain on South Dakota State Capitol Lake is fed by an artesian well with natural gas content so high that it causes it to glow.
2. The tradition of spreading sawdust on the floors of bars began in Deadwood as an effort to hide gold dust that would gather there.
3. Belle Fourche is the geographical center of the United States of America.
4. Mitchell is the home of the world's only Corn Palace, which is made of 3500 bushels of corn.
5. Mount Rushmore, also called the President's Mountain was constructed by Gutzon Borglum. The Crazy Horse mountain carving is the world's largest sculpture at 563 feet high, and 641 feet long.

Tennessee

State Name:	Tennessee
Capital:	Nashville
Abbreviations:	TN, Tenn.
Nickname:	The Volunteer State
Other Names:	Big Bend State; Mother of Southwestern Statesmen; Hog and Hominy State
Motto:	Agriculture and Commerce
Statehood:	June 1, 1796 (16th)
Demonym:	Tennessean
Time Zone:	Central Standard Time ; Eastern Standard Time
Region/Div:	South / East South Central
Slogan:	Volunteer State; Sounds Good to Me
Song:	"My Homeland, Tennessee"; "When It's Iris Time in Tennessee"; "My Tennessee"; "Tennessee Waltz"; "Rocky Top"; "Tennessee" (1992); "The Pride of Tennessee"; "Smoky Mountain Rain"; "Tennessee (2011)"
Name Origin:	The name may have been derived from a Cherokee town named Tanasi.
Brief History:	The first British settlement in what is now Tennessee was built in 1756 by settlers from the colony of South Carolina at Fort Loudoun, near present-day Vonore. In 1763, The British took control of the area from the French after the French and Indian War. In the 1772, the European formed the Watauga Association, a community built on lands leased from the Cherokee peoples. In 1784, the State of Franklin was established. However it ended in 1788. In 1796, Congress made Tennessee the 16th state of the United States. In 1861, Tennessee was the last of the southern states to secede from the Union and join the Confederacy. And in 1866, Tennessee was readmitted as a state in the Union.

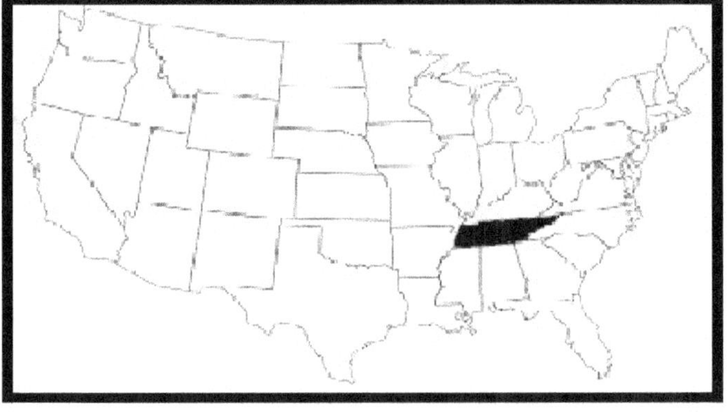

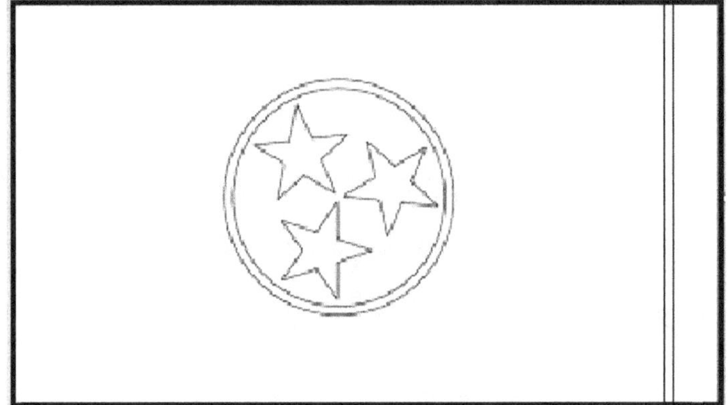

Flag

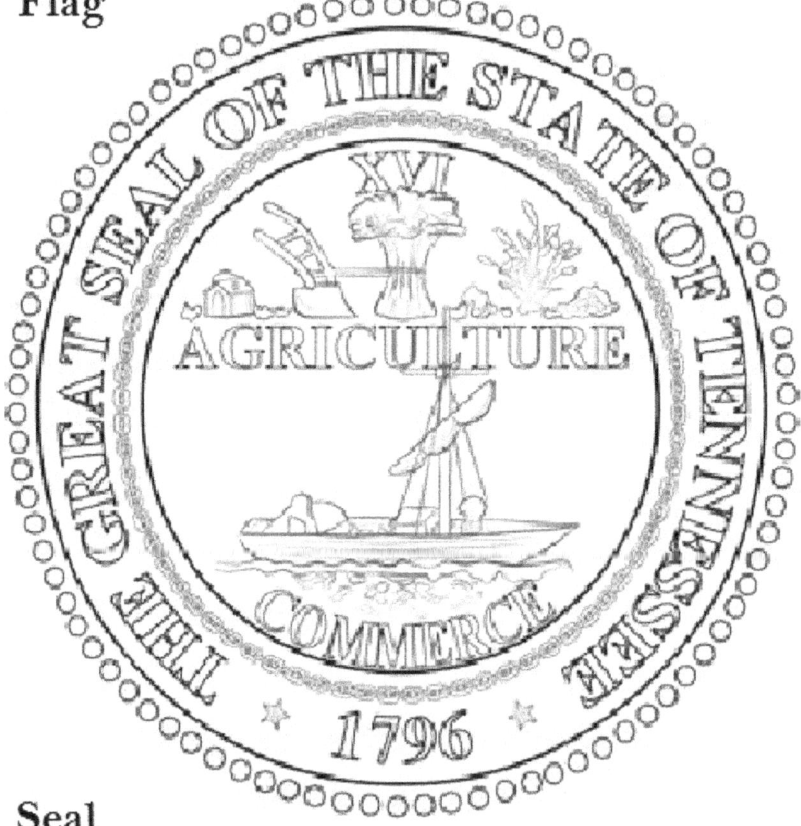

Seal

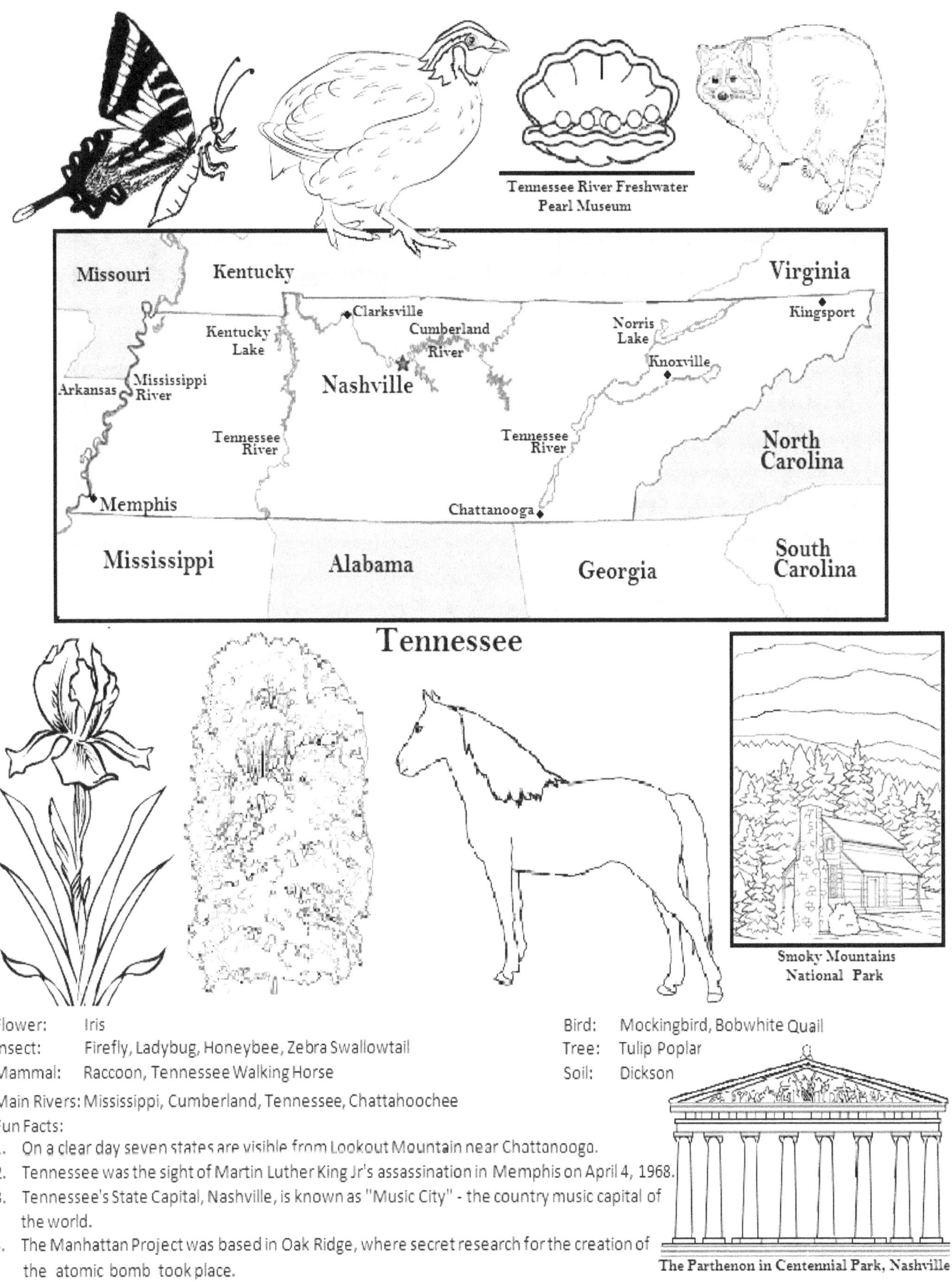

Flower: Iris

Insect: Firefly, Ladybug, Honeybee, Zebra Swallowtail

Mammal: Raccoon, Tennessee Walking Horse

Bird: Mockingbird, Bobwhite Quail

Tree: Tulip Poplar

Soil: Dickson

Main Rivers: Mississippi, Cumberland, Tennessee, Chattahoochee

Fun Facts:

1. On a clear day seven states are visible from Lookout Mountain near Chattanooga.
2. Tennessee was the sight of Martin Luther King Jr's assassination in Memphis on April 4, 1968.
3. Tennessee's State Capital, Nashville, is known as "Music City" - the country music capital of the world.
4. The Manhattan Project was based in Oak Ridge, where secret research for the creation of the atomic bomb took place.
5. The Lost Sea in Sweetwater is the largest underground lake in the United States and the second largest in the world.

Texas

State Name:	Texas
Capital:	Austin
Abbreviations:	TX; Tex.
Nickname:	The Lone Star State
Other Names:	Beef State; Super-American State; Remember the Alamo; The Blizzard State; The Jumbo State
Motto:	Friendship
Statehood:	December 29, 1845 (28th)
Demonym:	Texan
Time Zone:	Central Standard Time; El Paso and Hudspeth counties and part of Culberson County: Mountain Standard Time
Region/Div:	South / West South Central
Slogan:	The Lone Star State; Texas: It's Like a Whole Other Country; Don't Mess with Texas
Song:	"Texas, Our Texas"
Name Origin:	From the Caddo and Hasinais Indian word "tejas" meaning "friends" or "allies." Prior to gaining its independence, Texas was a province of Mexico named Coahuila y Tejas.
Brief History:	The Republic of Texas was formed in 1836, after breaking away from Mexico in the Texas Revolution. As early as 1837, the Republic made several attempts to negotiate annexation with the United States. Texas finally joined the union by treaty instead of territorial annexation in 1845 when the expansionist James K. Polk won the election of 1844.

Flag

Seal

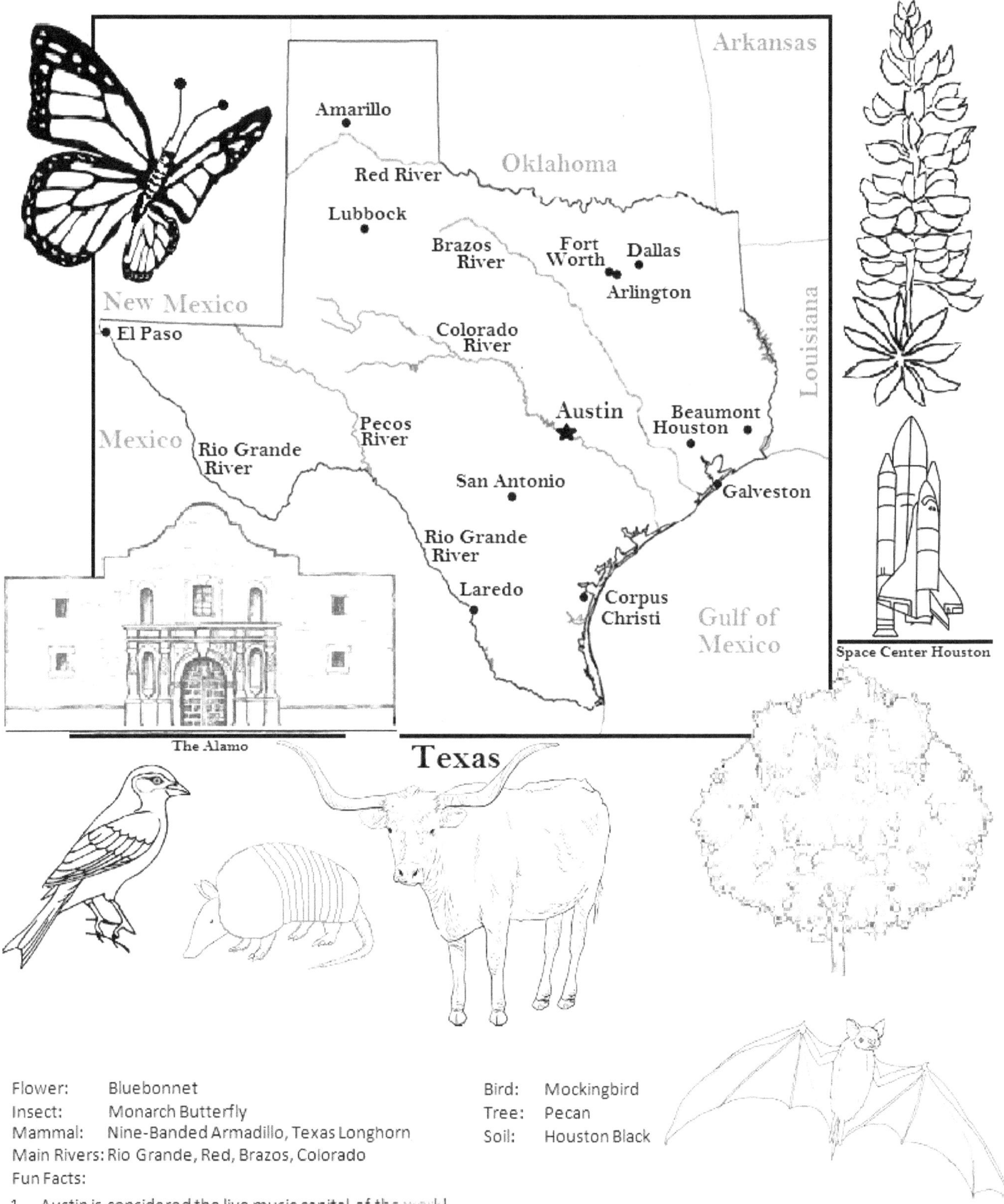

Flower: Bluebonnet
Insect: Monarch Butterfly
Mammal: Nine-Banded Armadillo, Texas Longhorn
Main Rivers: Rio Grande, Red, Brazos, Colorado

Bird: Mockingbird
Tree: Pecan
Soil: Houston Black

Fun Facts:

1. Austin is considered the live music capital of the world.
2. More bat species can be found in Texas than in any other state.
3. First covered stadium in the U.S. was constructed in Houston, in 1965.
4. Texas is the only state to have the flags of 6 different nations fly over it. They are: Spain, France, Mexico, Republic of Texas, Confederate States, and the United States.
5. The capitol in Austin opened May 16, 1888. The dome of the building stands seven feet higher than that of the nation's capitol in Washington, D.C.

Utah

State Name:	Utah
Capital:	Salt Lake City
Abbreviations:	UT; Ut.
Nickname:	The Beehive State
Other Names:	The Mormon State; Land of the Saints; Salt Lake State
Motto:	Industry
Statehood:	January 4, 1896 (45th)
Demonym:	Utahn
Time Zone:	Mountain Standard Time
Region/Div:	West / Mountain
Slogan:	Center Scenic America; This Is the Place; Ski Utah!; Greatest Snow on Earth
Song:	"Utah, We Love Thee"
Name Origin:	From the Ute tribe and it means "people of the mountains".
Brief History:	Utah was Mexican territory until it became part of the United States with the Treaty of Guadalupe Hidalgo that ended the Mexican-American War. The Territory of Utah was organized and it existed from September 9, 1850, until it was admitted to the Union.

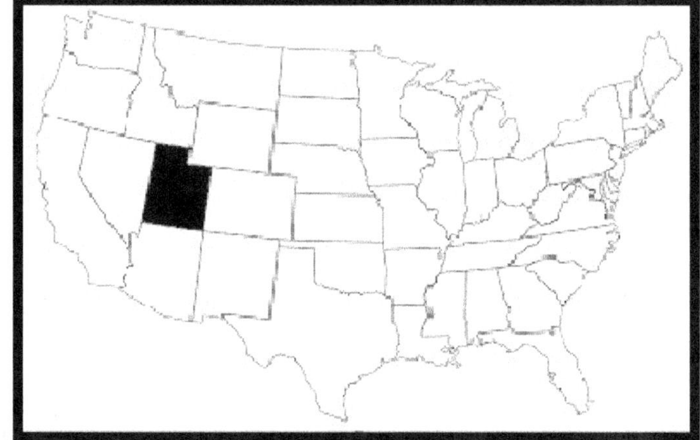

Flag

Seal

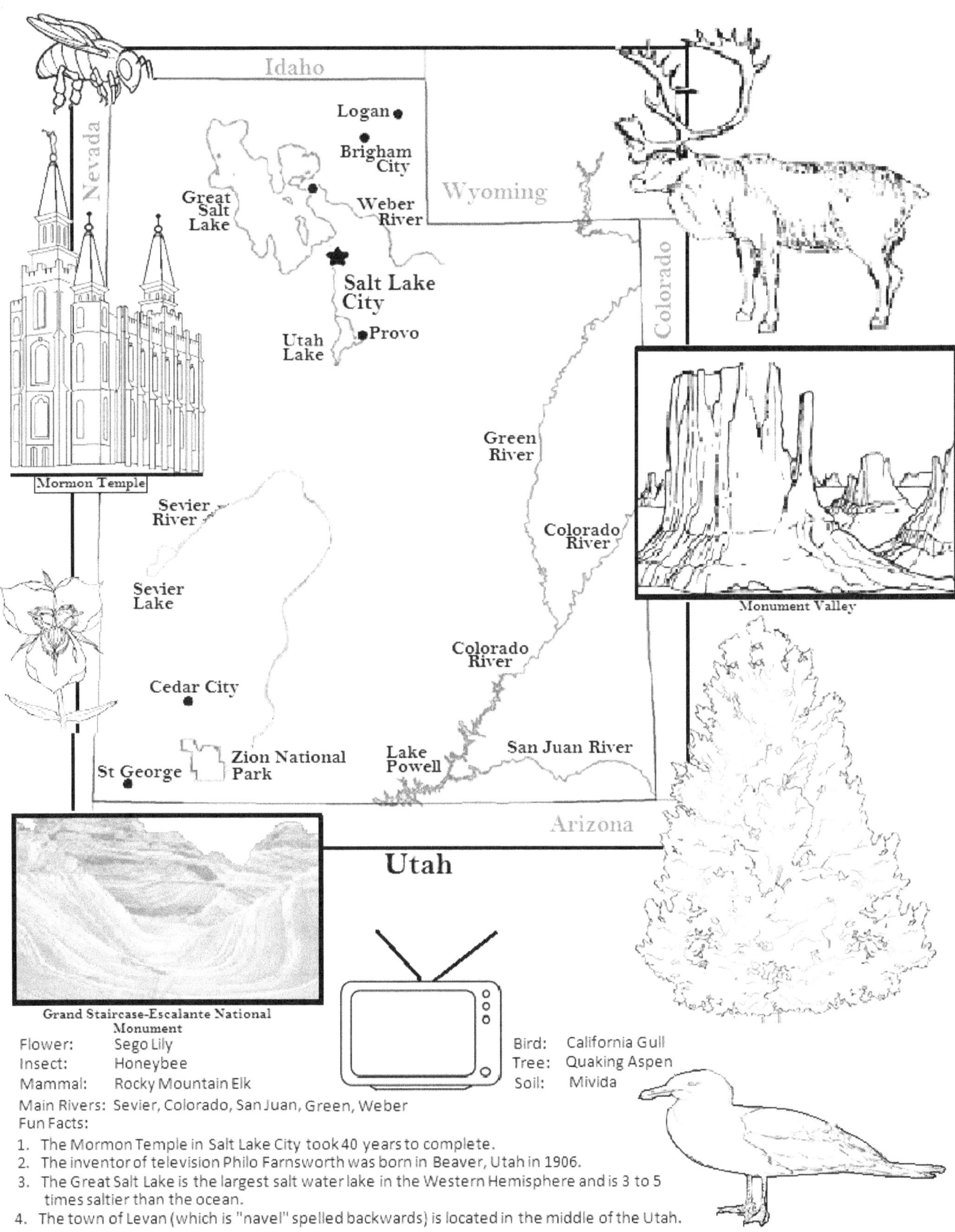

Flower: Sego Lily
Insect: Honeybee
Mammal: Rocky Mountain Elk
Main Rivers: Sevier, Colorado, San Juan, Green, Weber

Fun Facts:

1. The Mormon Temple in Salt Lake City took 40 years to complete.
2. The inventor of television Philo Farnsworth was born in Beaver, Utah in 1906.
3. The Great Salt Lake is the largest salt water lake in the Western Hemisphere and is 3 to 5 times saltier than the ocean.
4. The town of Levan (which is "navel" spelled backwards) is located in the middle of the Utah.
5. The Bonneville Salt Flats comprises 30,000 acres of desolate, densely packed salt pan, a popular destination for speed-seeking land racers.

Vermont

State Name:	Vermont
Capital:	Montpelier
Abbreviations:	VT; Vt.
Nickname:	The Green Mountain State
Other Name:	The Maple State
Motto:	Vermont, Freedom and Unity; May 14 star shine bright
Statehood:	March 4, 1791 (14th)
Demonym:	Vermonter
Time Zone:	Eastern Standard Time
Region/Div:	Northeast / New England
Slogan:	I LoVermont; Vermont, naturally; Vermont: The Boutique State with a Megastore Attitude
Song:	"Hail Vermont"; "These Green Mountains"
Name Origin:	An English form of the name that French explorer Samuel de Champlain gave to Vermont's Green Mountains on his 1647 map. He called the place "Vert Mont" meaning green mountain.
Brief History:	In 1609 Samuel de Champlain explored Vermont and claimed the land for France. In 1763, the British won the French and Indian War (1754-1763) and took control of Vermont through the 1763 Treaty of Paris. In 1777, Vermont became an independent republic. In 1791, the U.S. Congress admitted Vermont as the 14th state.

Flag

Seal

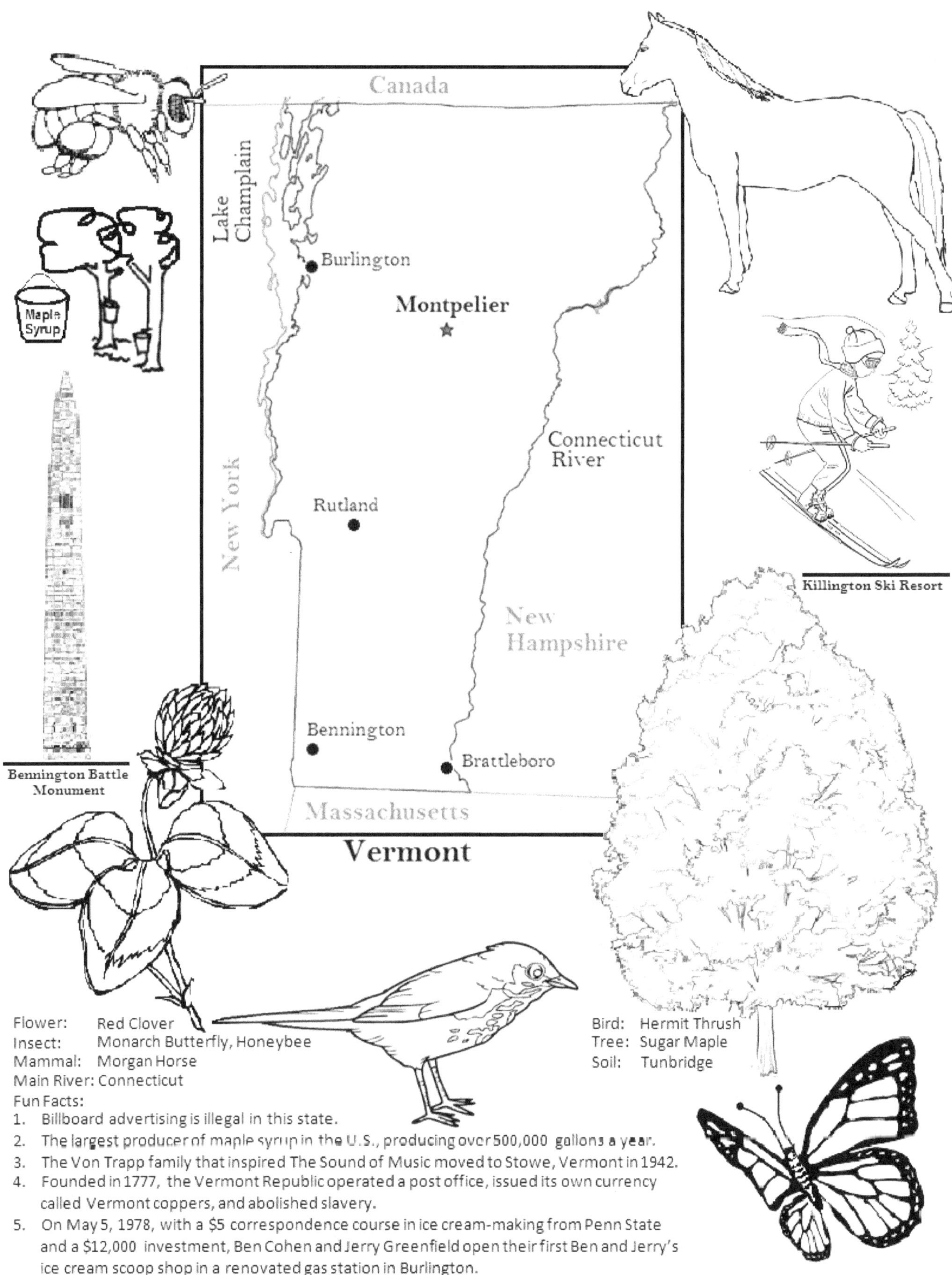

Flower: Red Clover
Insect: Monarch Butterfly, Honeybee
Mammal: Morgan Horse
Main River: Connecticut

Bird: Hermit Thrush
Tree: Sugar Maple
Soil: Tunbridge

Fun Facts:
1.   Billboard advertising is illegal in this state.
2.   The largest producer of maple syrup in the U.S., producing over 500,000 gallons a year.
3.   The Von Trapp family that inspired The Sound of Music moved to Stowe, Vermont in 1942.
4.   Founded in 1777, the Vermont Republic operated a post office, issued its own currency called Vermont coppers, and abolished slavery.
5.   On May 5, 1978, with a $5 correspondence course in ice cream-making from Penn State and a $12,000 investment, Ben Cohen and Jerry Greenfield open their first Ben and Jerry's ice cream scoop shop in a renovated gas station in Burlington.

Virginia

State Name:	Commonwealth of Virginia
Capital:	Richmond
Abbreviations:	VA; Va.
Nickname:	The Old Dominion
Other Names:	Mother of Presidents; Cavalier State; Mother of States
Motto:	Thus always to tyrants
Statehood:	June 25, 1788 (10th)
Demonym:	Virginian
Time Zone:	Eastern Standard Time
Region/Div:	South / South Atlantic
Slogan:	Virginia is for Lovers; Live Passionately; Where Love Lives
Song:	"Carry Me Back to Old Virginia"
Name Origin:	In honor of Elizabeth "Virgin Queen" of England

Brief History: In 1607, the Jamestown Colony was established by the Virginia Company of London. In 1624, the area became a British colony. In 1776, Thomas Jefferson from Virginia wrote the Declaration of Independence. In 1788, Virginia became the 10th state. In 1861, Virginia seceded from the Union and joined the Confederate States and the Civil War started. In 1863, West Virginia parted from Virginia and formed its own state. In 1870, Virginia was readmitted to the Union.

Flag

Seal

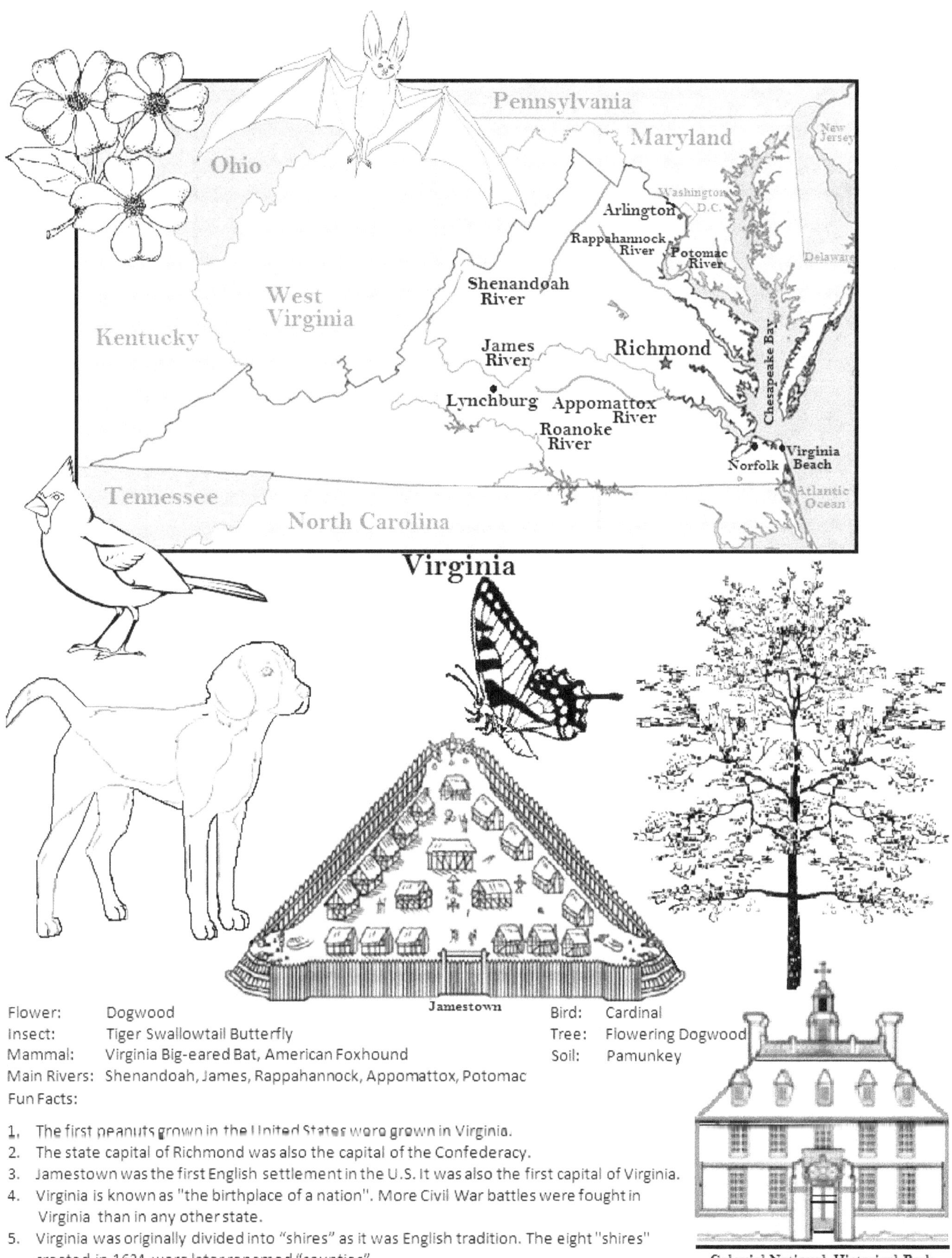

Flower:	Dogwood	Bird: Cardinal
Insect:	Tiger Swallowtail Butterfly	Tree: Flowering Dogwood
Mammal:	Virginia Big-eared Bat, American Foxhound	Soil: Pamunkey

Main Rivers: Shenandoah, James, Rappahannock, Appomattox, Potomac

Fun Facts:

1. The first peanuts grown in the United States were grown in Virginia.
2. The state capital of Richmond was also the capital of the Confederacy.
3. Jamestown was the first English settlement in the U.S. It was also the first capital of Virginia.
4. Virginia is known as "the birthplace of a nation". More Civil War battles were fought in Virginia than in any other state.
5. Virginia was originally divided into "shires" as it was English tradition. The eight "shires" created in 1634 were later renamed "counties".

Washington

State Name:	Washington
Capital:	Olympia
Abbreviations:	WA; Wash.
Nickname:	The Evergreen State
Other Names:	The Green Tree State; The Chinook State
Motto:	Al-Ki (Indian word meaning "by and by")
Statehood:	November 11, 1889 (42nd)
Demonym:	Washingtonian
Time Zone:	Pacific Standard Time
Region/Div:	West / Pacific
Slogan:	The Evergreen State
Song:	"Washington, My Home"
Name Origin:	In honor of George Washington

Brief History: In 1775, the Washington coast was sighted by Spanish Captain Don Bruno de Heceta and claimed the land for Spain. In 1778, the area was explored by Captain James Cook. In 1790, the Spanish Nootka Concession opened the northwest territory to explorers and trappers. In 1792, Spain established the first European settlement in Washington at Neah Bay. In 1819, Spain ceded their original claims to the territory to the United States. This began a period of disputed joint-occupancy by Britain and the U.S. In 1846, the Treaty of Oregon between United States and Great Britain sets the boundary at 49th parallel. In 1853, the Washington Territory was formed from part of the Oregon Territory. The Enabling Act of 1889 is a United States statute that permitted the admittance of Washington into the United States of America.

Flag

Seal

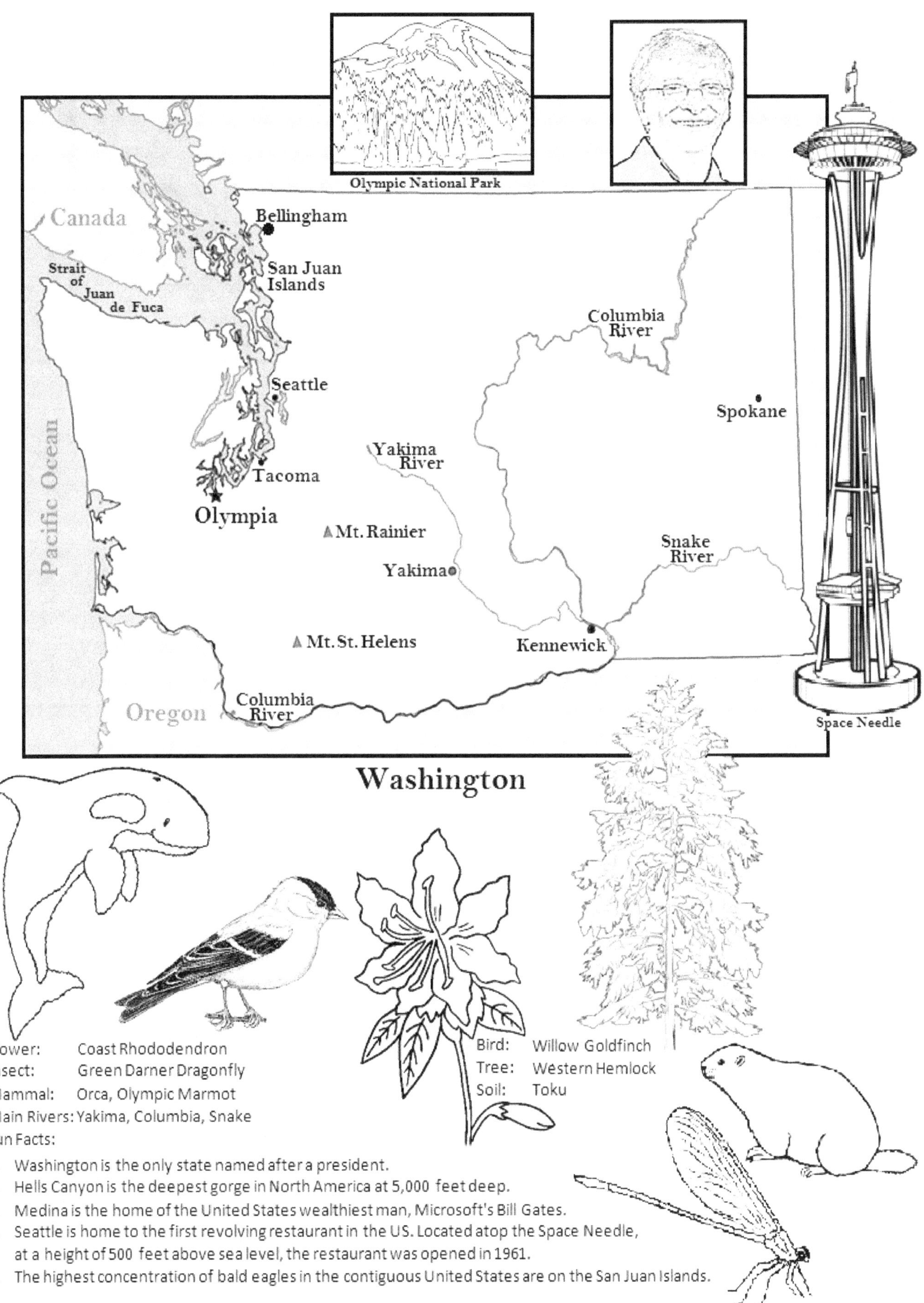

Washington

Flower: Coast Rhododendron
Insect: Green Darner Dragonfly
Mammal: Orca, Olympic Marmot
Main Rivers: Yakima, Columbia, Snake

Bird: Willow Goldfinch
Tree: Western Hemlock
Soil: Toku

Fun Facts:

1. Washington is the only state named after a president.
2. Hells Canyon is the deepest gorge in North America at 5,000 feet deep.
3. Medina is the home of the United States wealthiest man, Microsoft's Bill Gates.
4. Seattle is home to the first revolving restaurant in the US. Located atop the Space Needle, at a height of 500 feet above sea level, the restaurant was opened in 1961.
5. The highest concentration of bald eagles in the contiguous United States are on the San Juan Islands.

West Virginia

State Name:	West Virginia
Capital:	Charleston
Abbreviations:	WV; W.Va.
Nickname:	The Mountain State
Other Names:	Switzerland of America; Panhandle State
Motto:	Mountaineers are always free
Statehood:	June 20, 1863 (35th)
Demonym:	West Virginian
Time Zone:	Eastern Standard Time
Region/Div:	South / South Atlantic
Slogan:	Mountain State; Wild, Wonderful
Song:	"The West Virginia Hills"
Name Origin:	West Virginia was named in honor of Elizabeth, "Virgin Queen" of England. Until 1861 West Virginia was part of Virginia. Virginia was named to honor Queen Elizabeth of England often referred to as the "Virgin Queen".
Brief History:	In 1861, the United States became massively divided over slavery, leading to the American Civil War (1861–1865), the western regions of Virginia split with the eastern portion politically. In 1863, the western region was admitted to the Union as a separate state and was named West Virginia.

Flag

Seal

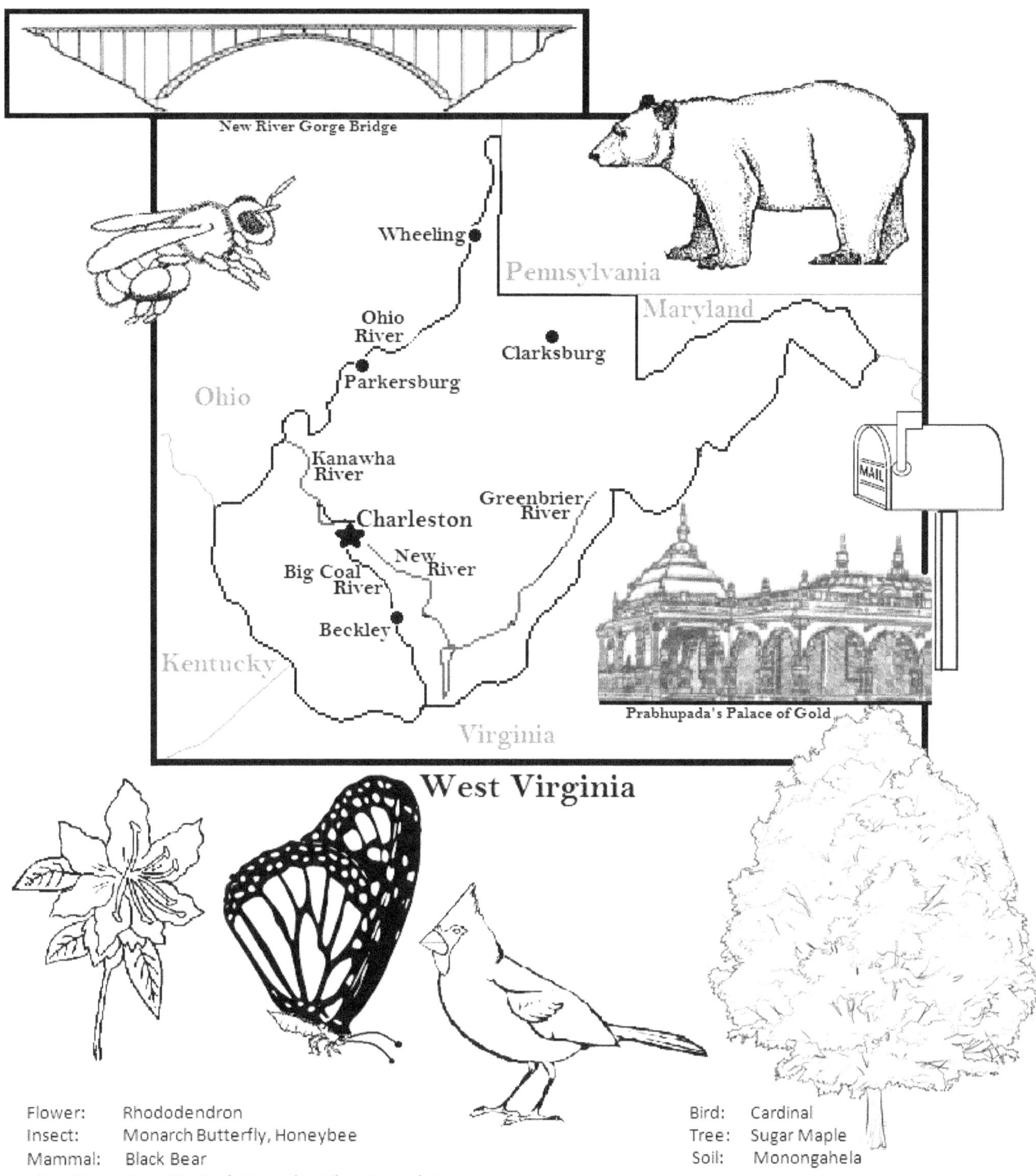

West Virginia

Flower: Rhododendron
Insect: Monarch Butterfly, Honeybee
Mammal: Black Bear

Bird: Cardinal
Tree: Sugar Maple
Soil: Monongahela

Main Rivers: New, Big Coal, Kanawha, Ohio, Greenbrier

Fun Facts:

1. West Virginia is considered the southernmost northern state and the northernmost southern state.
2. Declared a state by President Abraham Lincoln, West Virginia is the only state to be designated by Presidential Proclamation.
3. West Virginia's Memorial Tunnel was the first in the nation to be monitored by television. It opened November 8, 1954.
4. New River is actually one of the oldest rivers in the World and flows south to north, opposite from most rivers because it was formed before the mountains.
5. The first rural free mail delivery was started in Charles Town on October 6, 1896, and then spread throughout the United States.

Wisconsin

State Name:	Wisconsin
Capital:	Madison
Abbreviations:	WI; Wis.
Nickname:	The Badger State
Other Names:	The Copper State; Dairy State; America's Dairyland; Cheese State
Motto:	Forward
Statehood:	May 29, 1848 (30th)
Demonym:	Wisconsinite
Time Zone:	Central Standard Time
Region/Div:	Midwest /East North Central
Slogan:	America's Dairyland; Live Like You Mean It
Song:	"On Wisconsin"
Name Origin:	Originally spelled Mescousing by the French, and later corrupted to Ouisconsin. Most likely it came from a Miami word Meskonsing meaning "it lies red" or "river running through a red place".
Brief History:	In 1679, Frenchman Daniel Greysolon, Sieur du Luth claims the region for France. In 1763, Great Britain obtained the region in settlement of the French and Indian Wars. The British treated the former Indian allies of the French like conquered peoples, which led to the Pontiac Rebellion against the British. In 1774, the Quebec Act makes Wisconsin a part of Province of Quebec. In September 3, 1783, The Treaty of Paris is signed and the United States takes ownership of Wisconsin.

Flag

Seal

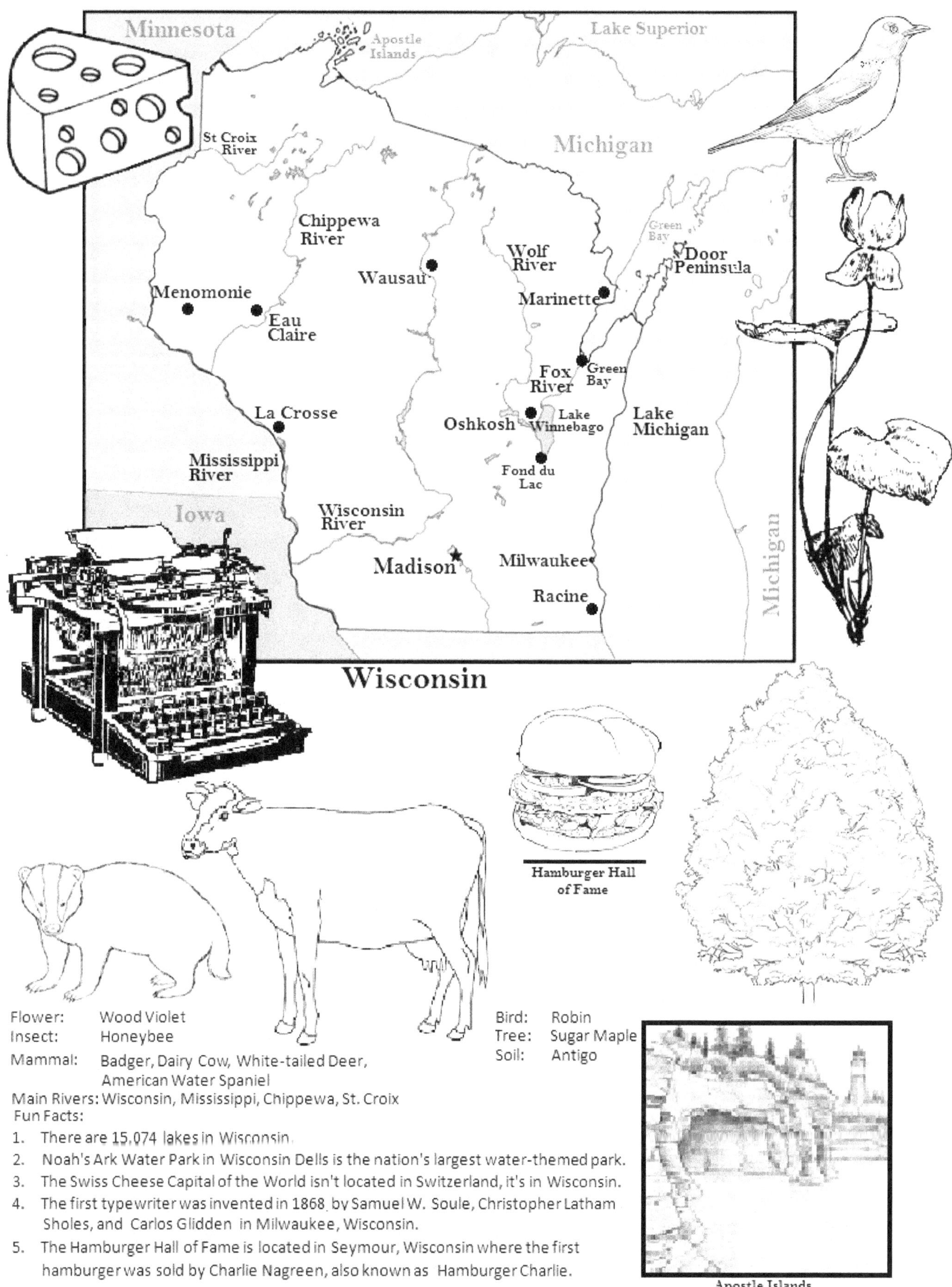

Flower: Wood Violet
Insect: Honeybee
Mammal: Badger, Dairy Cow, White-tailed Deer, American Water Spaniel

Bird: Robin
Tree: Sugar Maple
Soil: Antigo

Main Rivers: Wisconsin, Mississippi, Chippewa, St. Croix

Fun Facts:

1. There are 15,074 lakes in Wisconsin.
2. Noah's Ark Water Park in Wisconsin Dells is the nation's largest water-themed park.
3. The Swiss Cheese Capital of the World isn't located in Switzerland, it's in Wisconsin.
4. The first typewriter was invented in 1868 by Samuel W. Soule, Christopher Latham Sholes, and Carlos Glidden in Milwaukee, Wisconsin.
5. The Hamburger Hall of Fame is located in Seymour, Wisconsin where the first hamburger was sold by Charlie Nagreen, also known as Hamburger Charlie.

Apostle Islands

Wyoming

State Name:	Wyoming
Capital:	Cheyenne
Abbreviations:	WY; Wyo.
Nickname:	Equality State
Other Names:	The Suffrage State; The Sagebrush State; The Cowboy State
Motto:	Equal rights
Statehood:	July 10, 1890 (44th)
Demonym:	Wyomingite
Time Zone:	Mountain Standard Time
Region/Div:	West / Mountain
Slogan:	Wyoming: Like No Place on Earth; Wyoming: Wynot?
Song:	"Wyoming"
Name Origin:	From the Munsee word xwé:wamənk, meaning "at the big river flat".
Brief History:	What is now southwestern Wyoming became a part of the Spanish Empire and later Mexican territory of Alta California, until it was ceded to the United States in 1848 at the end of the Mexican–American War. The larger part of the state was acquired from France as part of the Louisiana Purchase in 1803.

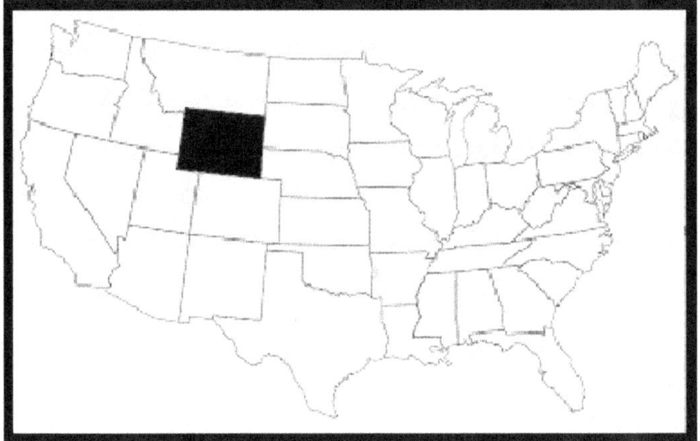

Flag

Seal

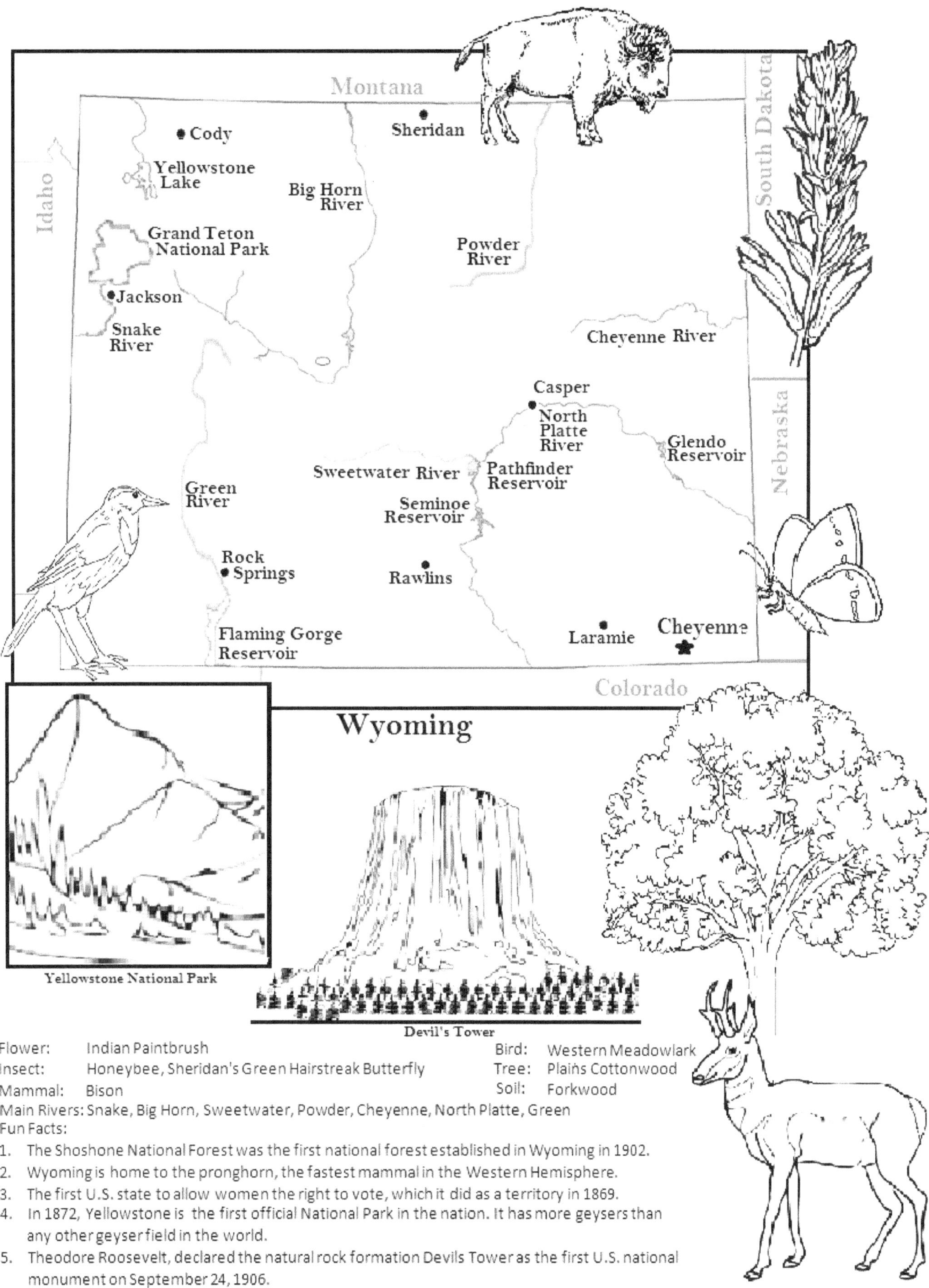

Yellowstone National Park

Devil's Tower

Flower: Indian Paintbrush

Insect: Honeybee, Sheridan's Green Hairstreak Butterfly

Mammal: Bison

Bird: Western Meadowlark

Tree: Plains Cottonwood

Soil: Forkwood

Main Rivers: Snake, Big Horn, Sweetwater, Powder, Cheyenne, North Platte, Green

Fun Facts:

1. The Shoshone National Forest was the first national forest established in Wyoming in 1902.
2. Wyoming is home to the pronghorn, the fastest mammal in the Western Hemisphere.
3. The first U.S. state to allow women the right to vote, which it did as a territory in 1869.
4. In 1872, Yellowstone is the first official National Park in the nation. It has more geysers than any other geyser field in the world.
5. Theodore Roosevelt, declared the natural rock formation Devils Tower as the first U.S. national monument on September 24, 1906.

ABOUT THE AUTHOR

M.L. Gutierrez is also the author of the following books:
The Bible Dilemma: Historical contradictions, misquoted statements, failed prophecies and oddities in the Bible
Flags of the United Nations, An adult and kid coloring book
Flags of the USA, An adult and kid coloring book
Flags of the World Series (Africa), adult coloring book
Flags of the World Series (America), adult coloring book
Flags of the World Series (Asia), adult coloring book
Flags of the World Series (Europe), adult coloring book
Flags of the World Series (Oceania and Antarctica), adult coloring book